W9-CAR-341

CONTEMPORARY
AFRICAN
ARTS and CRAFTS

CONTEMPORARY
AFRICAN
ARTS and CRAFTS

ON-SITE WORKING WITH ART FORMS AND PROCESSES

\\\\\\\\\\\\\\\\\\\

THELMA R. NEWMAN

\\\\\\\\\\\\\\\\\

CROWN PUBLISHERS, INC., NEW YORK

To all
the unknown artists and craftsmen of Africa,
my deepest appreciation

Inquiries should be addressed to Crown Publishers, Inc., 419 Park Avenue South, New York, N.Y. 10016.

Library of Congress Catalog Card Number: 73–91515

Printed in the United States of America
Published simultaneously in Canada by
General Publishing Company Ltd.

Designed by Ruth Smerechniak

ACKNOWLEDGMENTS

A book such as this, that looks at the art and craft of so many different people, owes its existence to these unknown artists and craftsmen. Appreciation also goes to Dr. Donald Wyckoff, executive vice president of the American Crafts Council, who arranged for contacts in West Africa. And to Mr. and Mrs. Daniel Cobblah of Accra, Ghana, goes especial gratitude. Daniel Cobblah's expertise is unmatched and he was completely open and giving. So were my hosts Kunle Oladipo of Oshogbo, Nigeria, and John N. Buer of Tamale, Ghana.

John Francis, head of the department of industrial design of the University of Science and Technology, Kumasi, Ghana, J. K. Amoah, Albert Berkoh, and J. Emofa were a veritable fund of information. Thanks also to J. K. Asante, Kente cloth weaver of Bonwire, Ghana, A. M. Bamford and his assistant, J. Apana of Bolgatanga, Ghana, Christian Debeneste and his agent Balla Sylla of Abidjan, Ivory Coast, and Pan Am in West Africa for their assistance.

It is almost impossible to have conceived of researching and writing this book without the assistance of my sons, Jay Hartley and Lee Scott Newman, who accompanied me on my trips to Africa, and my husband and "quartermaster general," Jack Newman.

Special thanks goes to Norm Smith for a dedicated and superb job of processing photos.

All photographs by the author or
her sons Jay Hartley and Lee Scott
Newman, unless otherwise noted.

"Whenever I have confronted that which was unfamiliar to me, I constantly sought neither to praise nor to condemn but only to understand."

—Spinoza

CONTENTS

∧∨∧∨∧∨∧∨∧∨∧∨∧∨∧∨∧∨∧∨
·'·'·'·'·'·'·'·'·'·

ACKNOWLEDGMENTS   V

PREFACE   xii

1 AFRICAN ARTS AS NONVERBAL
   COMMUNICATION   1
   Art as a Language   1
   Qualities of Pan-African Art   2
   Variations on the Theme of African Art   9
   Change of African Art Form   9
   History   11
   Geography   14
   People of Africa   14
   Kinds of Materials and Tools for Art   16
   Kinds of Art   16
   Castes of Society   17
   Ubiquitous Spirits   18
   Dress   19

2 THE POTTER'S ART   26
   Background   26
   Design and Use of Pottery   27
   Working with Clay   27
      Preparation of Clay   30
      Forming   30
      Drying   39
      Firing   39
      Decorating   49
   Try It   53

3 AFRICAN TEXTILE ARTS   58
  Background   59
  PART ONE *Decorating Fabrics*   66
  Resist Processes   66
    Preparing Indigo Dye   66
    Adire Eleso   69
    Adire Eleko   73
  Try It   78
  Printing Process—*Adinkra*   79
  Try It   89
  Painting on Cotton Cloth—Senufo Style   89
  Try It   96
  Appliqué   97
  PART TWO *Weaving*   102
  Preparing Cotton—Cleaning and Spinning   102
  Weaving   105
    Woman's Loom   105
    Raffia Weaving   108
    Man's Loom   110
  Try It   121

4 CONTAINERS: BASKETS AND CALABASHES   127
  Basketry   127
    Preparation of Materials   129
    Basketry Construction   139
  Try It   144
  The Calabash   147
    Preparing Calabashes (Gourds)   147
    Calabash Decoration   149
  Try It   164

5 HIDES, SKINS, AND FEATHERS   165
  Traditions   165
  Uses for Leather   166
  Processes   177
    Working with Leather   177
    Decorating Leather   186
  Try It   188

6 BEADS, SHELLS, AND BONES   193
  The Ubiquitous Bead   193

Kinds of Beads   197
Patterns of Beads   212
Processes   214
  Woven Beadwork   215
  Spot Stitching   217
  Netted Beadwork   218
  Lazy Stitching   219
  Shells and Bones   219
Try It   219

7 WORKING WITH METALS   224
History   224
Objects of Metal   227
Process   227
Try It   242

8 CARVING WOOD AND IVORY   245
Kinds of Carvings   245
Design and Expression   261
Makonde Carving   264
Thorn Carving   273
Ivory and Bone Carving   283
Process   286
Try It   291

BIBLIOGRAPHY   292

Map of Africa   294
Tribal Map   295

INDEX   299

PREFACE

∧∨∧∨∧∨∧∨∧∨∧∨∧∨∧∨∧∨∧

PROLOGUE

Once regarded as minor arts, decorative and craft forms now deserve major treatment because the old hierarchy that established paintings and sculptures on an exalted level is losing ground to a new awareness of the significance of craft forms. I question whether painting and sculpture are more eminently expressive of a people than, for instance, weaving or jewelry making. Why is a functional creation that draws on the same inventive skill of a people and mirrors their environment in material and design inspiration less important than a nonfunctional form? Does not art of a people, by the people, for people's use, share more of a common language and have as much meaning as a more rarefied art form?

After every art form, I have translated any variations or adaptations in the process for you to "Try It." This increases one's understanding of an art form. If there are few "Try It" suggestions, it is because the process is easily adapted without any modifications. The tendency, always, is to use natural materials and simple tools, except as in cire perdue, where elaborate or professional equipment is more advisable.

In the African context, useful objects certainly are more accessible to the untrained today (people in general) than, for example, sculpture as expressed in ancestor figures and masks. These forms of sculpture are disappearing from the scene, as old rituals are being replaced by new developments in science and technology. But textiles as they are expressed in dress, metal, and beads as they become adornment, are more significant, in an immediate sense, because not only do they describe what *is* African as sculptures did, but in a nonthreatening way they support and provide symbols for the Africans' quest for Africanness—national identity.

xii

CONTENT

Contemporary African Arts and Crafts does not distinguish between fine art and craft. To the African there is no art; what they fashion and express is just a part of their lives—whether it is fine art or craft. (I would rename this book, if I were sure that semantic differences in interpretation would not be misunderstood. A more fitting title, I think, would be *Contemporary African Arts.*)

What is contained in this book is, for the most part, a firsthand, on-site collection of art forms that still exist—but probably not for long in the case of some. A few examples clearly demonstrate the assimilation of technology as form and process. Other pieces still reside in the domain of tradition; some are crossing the border into the new era of a vital and viable Africa. These are forms that reflect today's Africa and will become tomorrow's tradition.

This is by no means a complete display. What we have tried to do here is survey a range of art of sub-Saharan Africa. To describe every form and process would require many volumes this size. As it was, it took several trips to Africa to gather the material shown here, sometimes under difficult conditions. But the people were so cooperative and delightful that difficulties in communication and transportation were substantially mitigated.

Not the least of our enjoyment came from an accruing appreciation of the skill and beauty evident in African craft forms—and the inventiveness of African craftsmen in applying meager resources to create these objects. That is one reason why process is highlighted here. We may appreciate the aesthetic qualities of a product, but to observe the process of creation is to understand more about the form.

The examples on these pages highlight beautiful African arts that should be more popularly known and shared with the world.

THELMA R. NEWMAN
September, 1973

"Author at Work," Fakaha, Ivory Coast.

1

ΛΛΛΛΛΛΛΛΛΛΛΛ

AFRICAN ARTS AS NONVERBAL COMMUNICATION

WWWWWWWWWW

ART AS A LANGUAGE

Like language and social organization, art is essential to man. As embellishment and as creation of objects beyond requirements of the most basic needs of living, art has accompanied man since prehistoric times. Because of its almost unfailing consistency as an element of many societies, art may be a response to some biological or psychological need. Indeed, it is one of the most constant forms of human behavior.

However, use of the word "art" is not relevant when we describe African "art," because it is really a European term at first growing out of Greek philosophy and later reinforced by European culture. The use of other terms such as exotic art, primitive art, *arts sauvage*, and so on, to delineate differences is just as misleading. Most such terms are pejorative—implying that African art is on a lower cultural level. Levels of culture are irrelevant here, since African and European attitudes toward the creative act are so different. Since there is no term in our language to distinguish between the essential differences in thinking, it is best then to describe standards of African art.*

⋀⋀

QUALITIES OF PAN-AFRICAN ART

African art attracts because of its powerful emotional content and its beautiful abstract form. Abstract treatment of form describes most often, with bare essentials of line, shape, texture and pattern, intense energy and sublime spirituality. Hundreds of distinct cultures and languages, and many types of people create over one thousand different styles that defy classification. Each art and craft form has its own history and its own aesthetic content. But there are some common denominators (always with exceptions).

African art is functional. Its function is its purpose whether it is economic, magical, or religious. There is, though, some art for its own sake, such as in the embellishment of pulleys used in weaving. The carving on the pulley may not make for a stronger pulley (a metal hook would be cheaper and stronger), but when asked why another kind wasn't used, the weaver answered, "One does not want to live without pretty things."

African art is a way of living the world. All its forms, whether masks, sculpture, houses, fabrics, pottery, poetry, music, or dance, render the invisible visible and reveal the meaning of the confrontation between life and death. (It was Paul Klee, influenced by African art, who said that the task of art was to make the invisible visible.)

The African artist works from the force to the form that embodies it. Until the twentieth century, European artists, inspired by Greek traditions, started from a concrete form, usually that of the human figure, to express the divine.

The African artist is not considered an artist. He may be a farmer who carves, or a smith who is endowed with magical powers. The responsibility for understanding the operation of forces issuing from

---

* Or to wait a few more years until the European concept of art more closely moves to the African's position on the meaning of what he creates.

Tribal heritage gave an African a sense of identity, pride, and security in belonging. This South African, a Xhosa from Peddie in Ciskei, is wearing handcrafted jewelry and fabrics made near and in his locale. He can associate closely with each piece—its process and heritage. *Courtesy: Smithsonian Institution*

African art is a way of living in the world. There is no distinction to the African between art and craft—what he uses, wears, and lives with. The Zulu from Zululand, South Africa (Hlabisa near Nongoma), are great masters at beadwork. They have achieved a high degree of artistry that to them is not art; it exists because it came before. *Courtesy: Smithsonian Institution*

the divine power, and of controlling them in a meaningful way, lies in the medicine man or priest. It is the priest who communicates the need for a certain form to the carver if it is to have some spiritual endowment. (That is why carvers don't see anything wrong in copying another carver's work. Copying is just a form of flattery.)

The African conception of art is a communal conception as compared with European individualistic expression. To the African, community existed prior to the individual and the individual is just a small part of a long tradition. This sense of unity extends to nature and to the earth—earth belongs to ancestors.

Secret societies, supporting the medicine man, maintain standards of behavior by special initiation tests, rituals for many occasions, oaths of secrecy, and the like. They supervise morality, uphold tribal traditions, and dispense justice. They set standards for art forms from birth through puberty, marriage, and death. Masks, sculptures in the form of ancestor figures, fetishes, and ritual implements (rattles and drums) conform to these traditions. Fetishes are objects endowed with magical powers for a specific purpose and are usually crudely fashioned by the medicine man.

African art gives form to the supernatural and invisible. Its abstract imagery does not even attempt to imitate concrete appearances. How does one represent the power and virtue of an ancestor, or the rhythm of an animal concretely? From this emerges a rhythmic unity and a reduction of every formal element to its eternal geometry.

African art is one that is in equilibrium with nature and forms a communion with nature. To the African, sculpture can be a receptacle of the ancestor's spirituality, and has the ability to transmit that spirituality when necessary. Its message or meaning becomes its presence.

African art is closer to life than is the art of other countries. Its art forms are within every man's reach. They are a necessity, an integral force, and part of living. As functional forms, they invite direct participation in their uses. This is the vitality in African art.

In summary, *African art explains the past, describes values and a way of life, helps man relate to supernatural forces, mediates* his social relations, expresses emotions and enhances man's present life as an embellishment denoting pride or status as well as providing entertainment* (dance, music).

---

* Among the Woyo, men usually eat with men but are served food by wives who deliver the food in a small pot covered with an unembellished wooden lid. If there is trouble between man and wife, the pot is covered with "programmatic" lids that serve to bring the disagreement into the open so that others can mediate and help settle it.

The conception of art to the African is a communal conception. The community existed prior to the individual person who is a small part of a long tradition. The community is the way it was. But this is changing in and near big cities. In more distant and isolated areas, however, life still is deeply rooted in tradition. This scene is from a village near Korhogo, Ivory Coast.

River people from along the coastal waterways of Dahomey.

A Masai from Tanzania, leaning against her dung-and-clay house.

A village north of Tamale, Ghana.

The young girl carrying two kinds of water jugs—a calabash and a polyethylene container; the man's traditional clothes and her European-type dress are indicators of the transition between traditional culture and the technological invasion that is widespread in Nigeria.

The sense of community, of people helping people, is still strong in Africa. Hairdressing is an art form in Korhogo, Ivory Coast.

/\.\./\.

VARIATIONS ON THE THEME OF AFRICAN ART

Common historical and environmental influences make for similarities, but there is also great diversity. Most social activity is marked by some art expression. Singing and dancing, although ubiquitous, do not exist among all tribes. Some Africans carve; others, though neighbors, do not. It may be that to the neighbor villager a piece of cloth with eyes and mouth cut into it suffices. Styles, therefore, vary from group to group. Every clan, every tribe, tries to represent ancestral beliefs or faith in a Supreme Being in its unique way, resulting in a great variation of art form.

/\.\./\.

CHANGE OF AFRICAN ART FORM

In all cultures, in varying degrees, art, as a language, has socially determined limits. However, formalized patterns of expression are constantly shifting. Today we accept forms that once were considered outlandish. A rarely gifted individual may dare to deviate and override traditional boundaries, thereby remapping and extending the acceptable range of expression. This shifting and changing of art form is a characteristic of more isolated and protected societies as it is of our own. Speed of acculturation, however, does vary.

But the speed and force of change may be accelerated by outside— indeed foreign—influences. Many years ago William Fagg wrote: "We are in at the death of all that is best in African art . . ." He was describing a well-known phenomenon in Africa. Patron kings had lost their power, rituals were dying out, carvers were putting down their tools. Art forms, though, flourish and die everywhere. This is not unique to Africa. New styles emerge from the fertile fields of the past. New identities are born. African art has been a vitalizing influence on European art. It inspired Picasso, Klee, Modigliani, Lipchitz, and others. Because of the influence of African art new images emerged in the art of Europeans. Influences of European art on African artists, on the other hand, were not necessarily disastrous either. Where African art was vital and powerful it did not die. Its richness, invention, and variety are still felt. African art is no more frozen in time than other art. There is a flow of style with time, and temporal changes are as real in Africa as they are elsewhere in the world. Today, in Africa, there are new styles in dress with new fabrics, batiks, embroideries, jewelry— that are not European but pan-African. African art is responding to these new influences, new clients are created, new needs and functions emerge. New forms are born.

People creating the art today may not be the sons and daughters of tradition. Some ceremonies are gone, but new artists are emerging who incorporate tradition into a contemporary imagery that engenders as much emotion, power, and vitality as traditional forms did. Why not use the new aniline dyes that are easier to mix than indigo? Cement is stronger than wood, mud, and straw and resists termites. It is a longer lasting building material.

There have been guilt feelings, though, that are not easy to resolve. The foreign triumvirate of missionary, politician, and trader did much to change life-styles and art styles of Africans because this suited their own ends. But it would not have happened if there were not a readiness for change of the old forms. The court art of Benin, for instance, declined long before the disastrous destruction by the British of Benin City in 1897. (But a beautiful record of history was lost.) Old Oyo, the ancient capital of Yoruba, was unable to control its vast slave population, and rebellious slaves established their own rival city of Ilorin. Then with the help of northern Muslims they invaded and destroyed the capital. In Dahomey, the religious rites of human sacrifice had turned into bloodthirsty orgies.

The pagan god too was an unyielding one—a difficult god. He had to be wooed constantly. Any false step unsettled the balance and results were disastrous. The sense of responsibility for those who manipulated and administered relationships between men and gods was overwhelming. Other "new" gods were much easier to live with. Islam and Christianity showed goodwill toward mankind. This was assured just for belief and obedience.

Traders came in and swamped local markets with manufactured goods and drove local craftsmen out of business. Japanese enamelware replaced carved calabashes. Lancashire cotton goods ousted the hand weaver, almost to the degree that they had in England. And pottery sometimes was replaced by polyethylene. The trader had to build up markets.

Some tribes such as the Bushmen avoided confrontation and moved deeper into the desert. Others accepted new forms, particularly when the divine king lost his power to the politician (who achieved independence and power from colonial government). Some assimilated new ideas and, with their heritage from tradition, evolved new personal yet African forms.

When the Ashanti king lost his power, his subjects took to weaving robes with royal patterns. If this had happened earlier, it would have cost a man his life. Traditional carvers became carpenters or formed co-ops to provide tourist art. Some emptily reproduce in assembly-line fashion the forms of tradition without care or conviction. Others cynically forge forms to imitate antiques by burying them in mud. Yet fine pieces of sculpture still are created. The Makonde, for instance, who migrated from Mozambique to Tanzania, refused to standardize their work and today create marvelous nonstereotyped forms from hardwood. The shape each piece takes is inspired by the wood grain or an inner feeling.

People who dwell along the old camel route of Mali, Upper Volta, the northern sections of Ivory Coast, Ghana, and Nigeria, still create their traditional crafts, live in the same type of house, and wear the same style of clothing that their ancestors did. Nomadic tribes such as the Masai preserve their indigenous styles. Their lives still center on their cattle herds—food, clothing, and shelter are cattle by-products. Only a few objects such as safety pins, needles, and beads are bought or bartered.

Social styles persist. A man's worth may still be determined by how many cattle he owns and then by how many brides he can afford to buy. He will still have to live in a multiple dwelling, eat, dress, and sleep very much as did his forefathers. If he moves to a city, he loses his regional identity to the universal life-style. Only with relatively slight variation does technologically supported culture vary. This is as true of Africa's art as it is of the art of other countries where technology displaced men in their own countries by alienating them from their indigenous culture.

HISTORY

The most ancient period of African history was one of a close bond with southern Mediterranean peoples. When the Sahara became a

To the Mexican, this is the eye-of-God, but to the Hausa of Northern Nigeria (where this was found) the meaning has been lost. This old woolen weaving is one link from the camel route of the past, where trading extended from the Mediterranean sea to south of the Sahara carrying with it aspects of culture. The Moors might have brought this symbol to Spain, and the Spanish, to Mexico.

waterless waste, isolation began. Clues to these ancient links have been discovered in rock paintings and drawings in the Tassili Plateau of the Atlas Mountains in the Fezzan. A French team under Henri Lhoti discovered and copied prehistoric paintings preserved in caves and canyons. These paintings held many clues; one painting depicted masks much like those of the Senufo people of the Ivory Coast. It suggested that these people lived farther north and were driven south in search of water. There were resemblances to other people as well. Theory has it that as the Sahara lost its rainfall the area turned into a formidable barrier separating the people of North Africa from those who moved south.

Egypt at one time was influenced and governed by the Kingdom of Kush (Ethiopia to the Greeks), which extended southwest to Axum and Punt—the Ethiopia and Somali of today. These areas provided slave labor, gold, ivory, ebony, and other exotic woods, gums, perfumes, ostrich feathers, precious stones, and skins of animals.

In Meroë were large deposits of iron ore and the technology to utilize it. The Meroitic culture was intermixed with influences from Egypt and Kush. The lion was a symbol for the Meroitic god Apedemek, a symbol that appears again and again as a symbol of royalty. Pottery was hand-molded by women in the same styles and by the same techniques found in West Africa today. Meroë was a major stop of the caravan routes along the Athara River leading to the Abyssinian highlands. These caravans also traversed the area between the Nile and Niger rivers. Another route lay across the Sahara from the shores of the Mediterranean to Gao on the Niger. There were the Selima Trail in the east, the Belma and Gadames trails to Lake Chad and Kano, and the Taodeni Trail to Timbuktu and Djenne in the middle Niger region. Culture was transmitted along these routes.

The people of the ancient kingdom of Ghana, much farther north than the Ghana of today, had learned iron skills from Meroë. They developed pointed iron weapons to go along with it and power from this arsenal. Luxury and an elegant life existed for the court of the divine king. His riches were salt and gold. Taste for luxury lead to the development of cire perdue, filigree work, elaborate weavings of silk, wool, and cotton, leatherwork, and pottery.

Until the fifteenth century the ancient trade routes sufficed, but by 1441 the Portuguese found a way to reach the west coast of Africa (Cape Verde), and by 1471 they found the Gold Coast—and gold. Further exploration brought the Portuguese to the royal court of Mbangakongo on the Congo River. And with Portuguese connections, European ships sailed to set up trading posts along the Atlantic coast between Cape Verde and the southern desert.

Some powerful kingdoms emerged—the kingdom of Ashanti, the Yoruba state of Oyo ruling over Benin and the rest of Yorubaland. Along the west coast were common cultural attributes of language, divine kingship, and pagan religion. Salt-gold trade and the bartering of slaves brought great wealth to the divine kings, and along with it new tensions and relationships with other kingdoms and the trading countries. Firearms and political play by colonial powers brought chaos and dissension to whatever part of Africa they touched. No longer was change slow and evolving but disturbing and displacing.

/\\.\\/\\
GEOGRAPHY

Africa is a land of great topological variety. There are savannahs and deserts, and the Great Rift Valley (formed in the glacial period when East Africa was split all the way from the Red Sea to Zambezi by a mighty fissure in the earth's crust). There are lakes and waterfalls, volcanoes, and snow-capped mountains of 20,000 feet, various vegetation from the primeval jungle to the vast salt steppe of the Kalahari Desert. There are great rivers such as the Nile, Congo, Niger, and Zambezi. Commensurately, the climate is pleasant and healthy to enervating and unbearable.

/\\.\\/\\
PEOPLE OF AFRICA

Ethnologically most of the people of Africa are of the black race, made up of Negro and non-Negro groups. The oldest African people are the nomadic *Bushmen* who mainly live in the south and west and in South Africa in the region of the Kalahari Desert. The *Negritos*, or *Pygmies*, were also nomadic and inhabit Central Africa, north to east of the Congo in the region of the Ubangi River and Gabon. The great *Negro* group has linguistic forms and physical features that are similar.

Architects of destruction are the ubiquitous termites of Africa. This is one of their self-made monuments. This scene is January in northern Tanzania.

They lived in West and Central Africa, east of Ethiopia. Tribes such as the Bambara, Zande, Mongbetu, Ashanti, Fanti, Ga, Yoruba, Ewe, Bini, Ibo, Ekoi, and others, are Negro. The *Bantu* are another group united by a common language. They inhabit East, Central, and South Africa. The Bakuba, Barundi, and Makonde Bukota are some Bantu tribes living in Kenya, Tanzania, Bambia, Botswana, and Lesotho. Still another group are the *Hamitic* people, the Berbers, Tuareg, Fulani, Somali, and so on. It is thought that they originally came from Asia Minor, and belong to the Caucasian, or white, race. The Nilo-Hamites and Nilotes are another group who live in Northeast and East Africa, mainly in Kenya and Tanzania, and belong to the Buganda, Masai, Suk, Turkana, and Karmojong tribes.

Some of these groups have intermarried, but broad cultural patterns predominate.

KINDS OF MATERIALS AND TOOLS FOR ART

One can imagine that a great diversity would emerge from so many different types of people. The heterogeneity among people and their contrasting geography made for selection of many diverse kinds of materials. Most objects initially are of vegetable origin, predominantly wood. But calabashes, fruit stones, fibrous bark, raffia, cotton, reeds, rattan, bamboo, and resins are commonly employed. Animal materials that are utilized are horn, skins, wool, feathers, shells, ivory, and teeth. Minerals used are bronze, brass, iron, aluminum, stone, clay, glass, dyes, and less frequently because of export needs to balance trade—gold and silver.

Tools are few and simple. The adz, chisel, and knife are used in carving; the poker, tongs, and pliers for metalwork, simple two- and four-harness looms for weaving, an improvised wheel, stones and corncobs for pottery. Knives, sticks, straw, and dies carved of calabashes are used to apply pastes and dyes. Even where carvers have formed a cooperative to turn out identical products, the tools and processes are traditional.

KINDS OF ART

The needs of a region and the kinds of materials used are closely related to the geography. Generally, in and near tropical forests, huts are built of wood; walls and floors are covered with mats ornamented with complicated geometrical designs. Objects are hung on walls or stand on mats. Grassland homes are of dried clay, sculptural in effect and adorned with carvings and all sorts of decorative articles. Calabashes, baskets, and ceramic pots are arranged in the courtyard. It is not uncommon to see woven straw ornaments adorn an interior courtyard wall. Some south African groups decorate their clay walls with geometric shapes defined in earth colors. In the Sudan, houses are rich in design. There are bowls and carved wooden dishes placed on decorated pottery stands. Clay pots, dishes, and baskets are covered with geometric designs.

These objects for everyday use, decorations on and for houses, mats, cooking utensils, clothing, stools, boxes, baskets, and bowls show a very sensitive feeling for form but have no apparent religious significance as do wood carvings of ancestor portraits, magic figures, fetishes, and masks. Carved masks or figures are regarded highly in relation to other goods, not only because of the degree of skill needed but because of the magical nature of the carving. Often a person who orders a mask or figure has to sacrifice to get it. Paying a high price increases the importance of the figure or mask.

The person who carves may be a farmer by trade. But, if there is a great demand for his work he is released from his share of labor in the fields and is paid with food, goats, or even a girl to carry out his work. His rewards are generous.

Social position in Africa depends upon a man's role and the form of culture to which his village belongs. Some skills rate higher in the eyes of certain people. Almost universally, though, a smith has a distinctive status. He strikes fires and creates essential tools such as plows and knives. But even more profoundly, the success of these tools (whether their products are bountiful or meager) depends upon occult forces. A smith, therefore, can be a very dominant and powerful person. To the Bantu of the Congo, a smith can become an adviser to a king, become a prince, or even achieve kingship.

CASTES OF SOCIETY

Some Africans believe that man's fundamental gifts are left to his successor at his death. Even his tools are said to contain his magic. At the very least they are endowed with some of his skills. Not only is succession as to who inherits his tools and his status predetermined, but a caste system rigidly defines social order, in the first place. It establishes who can do what. Associations and organizations maintain this order. Not long ago a man could not become a carver or smith because he had the talent (there was no admission that talent existed). Nor could a man become a potter; it was a woman's job. Nor could a woman become a weaver, because it was a man's job, with the exception of weaving certain kinds of cloth. This is changing. (I met a very important male ceramist in Ghana, Daniel Cobblah. His grandmother was a potter.)

/.\./\.\

UBIQUITOUS SPIRITS

This world, for the African, is twofold—visible and invisible. The visible world is made up of people and things one can see. The invisible world is a world filled with spirits. Spirits are ubiquitous. They reside in everything because they need to emerge from the dream or imaginary world as a material object. Therefore, they may live in a figure, mask, mineral, or vegetable concoction. The object becomes a temporary home for a spirit. After a while, spiritual qualities seep away and confidence in the object decreases. Then, a new spirit approaches a man in his dreams and it asks to be carved by a carver.

South of the Sahara the mask is an agent of social control. A wearer of a mask and its attached raffia costume is an apparition of a super-human emerging from the bush. Masks are used by many tribes to guard boys against evil in the bush during initiation. There might be evil influences of people who would wish misfortune, and boys need protection. The mask once was essential to keep law and order. Spirits residing within a mask made the need for policemen in a chiefdom unnecessary. There are also masks used for entertainment. These may be classed as good masks and can be mischievous, both in a positive and negative sense.

Except for daily objects of use around the household, almost every activity is controlled by spirits in some way. African dolls, the kind carried by girls, are not ordinary playthings, but forms imbued with magic. For that reason they must be protected and cherished. The Moran, a warrior class of Masai, use a shield made of buffalo or giraffe hide. The design is abstract but has had definite meanings (which have been forgotten). Color, though, is still important. The background is usually white chalk with drawings of black (pumpkin rind burned into a charcoal), with blue and sometimes with some red (fruit juice or blood) areas. Only the Moran may use red. Although exact meanings are lost, design still denotes rank and status.

Naomi of Weija, Ghana, throwing a pot.

Frafra basket by Apana of Bolgatanga, Ghana, on an indigo dyed *adire eleso* (tie-dyed) cloth from Oshogbo, Nigeria.

Dogon carved wooden mask of Mali.

Kente cloth by Ashantis of Bonweri, Ghana, called *sika futwru* (gold dust).

Appliqué describing a historical story of a warrior hero from the Aizo region of Dahomey called Dako.

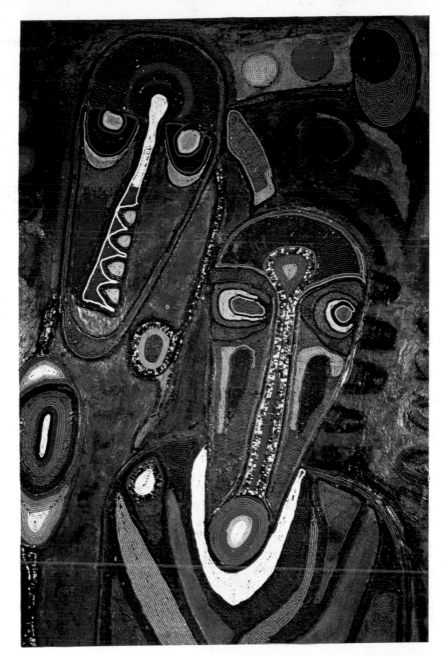

also pp- 21 + 122

A painting in oil and beads by Jimoh Buraimoh of Oshogbo, Nigeria.

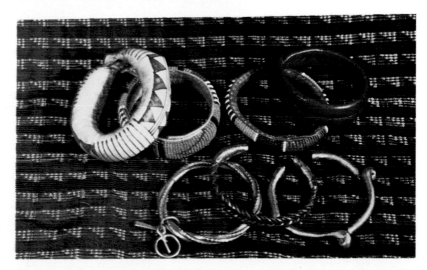

Assorted bracelets in leather, beads, and bronze in the lost wax process made by Africans from East and West Africa.

Fabric, beads, and seeds cover the wood foundation of this doll by the Bamum people of Cameroun.

Adire eleko, a cassava paste resist, indigo-dyes cotton textile from Oshogbo, Nigeria.

A Tuareg man's leather wallet-purse from Mali.

Raffia woven basket tray from Kano,
Nigeria.

Senufo fabric painting from Fakaha, Ivory
Coast.

Tuareg straw-over-wax necklaces that imitate
gold.

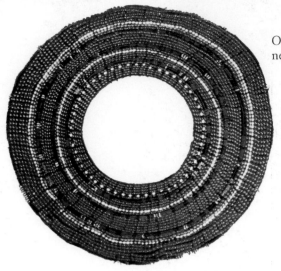

Old beaded Masai ceremonial dance necklace from Tanzania.

Straw wall ornaments from Mali.

This painted leather-covered basket by the Tuaregs of Timbouctou, Mali, is used to store sugar.

Two carved wooden stools, inlayed with beads from Kenya.

A large carved calabash from Iwo, Nigeria.

A leather bolster with designs cut and peeled from the skin. From Korhogo, Ivory Coast.

Reed necklace, probably of the Kamba or Turkana people of Kenya.

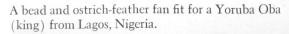
A bead and ostrich-feather fan fit for a Yoruba Oba (king) from Lagos, Nigeria.

A very large, five-foot, ceremonial mask from Boko Nle, Upper Volta. Colors are made from terra-cotta clay, kaolin, and charcoal.

Woven raffia hunting bags of the Bamileke people of Cameroun.

/.\./\.\

DRESS

Dress meets society's requirements, for both modesty and fashion. Fashion varies immensely from area to area. The Yoruba of Nigeria dress very differently from the Masai of Tanzania, or the Pygmies of the Congo. Although dress for male city dwellers is becoming predominantly European, there is a great deal of pressure on women to maintain indigenous dress styles. These regional variations are becoming pan-African and losing a great deal of former tribal identity. As to the sameness of dress, such as how a woman wraps fabric about her body, no two fabrics appear to be alike—indeed the variety is tremendous.

Propriety, prestige, or prerogative has little to do with comfort. Some groups can wear thirty pounds of iron on their legs. Wearing anklets requires Ibo women of high status to waddle. Huge, heavy-beaded collars eighteen inches in diameter used by the Masai in dance restrict the body to a certain posture and movement. Complete nudity is rare, except for prepuberty. Some body covering is used, even if it is minimal.

Scarification is a form of dress and decoration. But more than white man's tattooing, cicatrization is a device for marking the permanency of a person's role and his origins as reflected in the permanency of the scar. Actually, it is caused by cutting little patterns on the skin, usually on face, breast, stomach, or back. When the tissue heals, it forms raised scars. Some scarification is also used as a plea to the gods. The Gheba cut three strokes at the corners of both eyes and the mouth as a plea to the gods to spare the child. The Masai, Turkana, and others pierce ears for hanging beaded ornaments, some heavy enough to cause holes as big as golf balls. Others pierce lips and noses for ornaments. Body and face painting is another distinction. Most of these decorative forms are disappearing. Some have been outlawed by government. But in remote, isolated regions, scarification and other forms of decoration continue, certainly, for the celebration of religious rites; the substitute for scars is makeup that can be washed away.

Hairstyle is another way the African woman individualizes herself. Braiding can be highly complex with all kinds of geometric forms and arrangements. For some tribes, the male also is adorned with an elaborate hairstyle: some of the hair is woven with other materials or plastered with clay. Hairstyles can be so complex, take so long to create, that the

same ones are worn for months. A special wooden pillow holds the head
in place when the wearer is at rest so that the hairstyle is not disturbed.
Here again comfort is subordinated to style and custom. Beauty predominates.

CONTEMPORARY ART
THAT HAS TRANSCENDED TRADITION

This is an example of traditional influence expressed in a contemporary idiom by Twins Seven Seven of
Oshogbo, Nigeria. The picture is drawn with watercolor, crayon, and India ink on brown kraft paper
and is based upon folklore and legend.

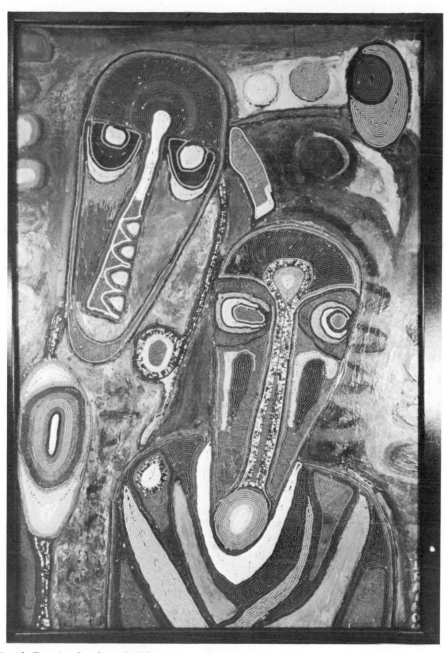

Jimoh Buraimoh, also of Oshogbo, works with oil paint and beads. His beads seem to reflect the glorious bead forms of the Yoruba as well as some traditional symbolism found in African masks.

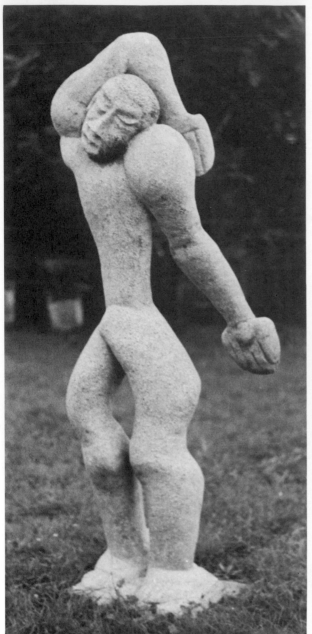

Stone sculptures by Oku Ampofo, a medical doctor
from Mampong Akwapim, near Accra, Ghana.

A gold pin made in the lost-wax process, using the symbolism of Ghanaian tradition, by E. Torto Johnson, a goldsmith of Dodowa, Ghana.

Susanne Wenger, a European, who has lived in Oshogbo, Nigeria, for many years, has been interested in religious symbols, dreams, fairy tales of the Yoruba. These images are syncretized in her work as shown in these two aspects of a fence and stairway in front of her home in Oshogbo.

2

∧∧∧∧∧∧∧∧∧∧∧∧

THE POTTER'S ART

∨∨∨∨∨∨∨∨∨∨∨∨

BACKGROUND

An Ivory Coast African legend about the origin of the universe has it
that a demiurge, probably a relative of the divine potter of Indo-Eu-
ropean myth, fashioned all living beings and all things from a primordial
material, the earth. Indeed, pottery is one of the earliest crafts, certainly
dating back to Africa's neolithic period when man used polished stone as
tools. Pottery was discovered in the sixth millennium B.C. in the Middle
East at Jericho in Palestine and spread to parts of North Africa. South
of the Sahara the earliest pottery found dates back to the fourth millennium B.C.

People of the Nok culture of northern Nigeria created pottery sculpture of nearly life size. These forms were transmitted to Ife (Yoruba
culture), and exhibited many of the qualities of the lost-wax-process
decorations like those appearing on bronze and shapes of heads on
offering bowls related to bronze forms of Benin.

26

The Ibo fashioned red clay figure groups and placed them in a shrine to serve as guardian spirits for the dead. In southern Ghana, terra-cotta heads and freestanding figures on pot lids are part of the funeral of an important person. These figures are formed only by men or old women past childbearing age. It is thought that if a young woman did this work, her fertility would be impaired or destroyed.

The Bakongo create figure-shaped pottery vessels. The Ashanti and Cameroon grasslands people fashion clay pipes. Walls of Bakuba huts are hung with groups of pots attached to the framework.

/\·\·/\
DESIGN AND USE OF POTTERY

Indeed, pots are formed all over Africa and are seen in every market. Africans cook in them, use them for storage, as dye pots for fabrics, as tubs for bathing babies. Huge sixty-quart porous unglazed pots are utilized as "refrigerated" water containers. Water keeps cool due to the evaporation of water on the surface of these pots.

Clay pots last for centuries, and yet can be very fragile. One of the reasons for the indigenous round shape of most pots is that clay is easier to form this way. A round shape increases the strength of otherwise fragile clay. Pottery increases in strength when corners are eliminated because there is less exposed surface in proportion to the capacity than in a square shape.

/\·\·/\
WORKING WITH CLAY

Clay is one of the most abundant substances on earth; nature makes it at a rate faster than all potters in the world can consume it. It is cheap, easily acquired and prepared, and does not require extensive processing as do most raw materials. Most clay in Africa (and elsewhere) results from hundreds of centuries of weathering of granite or feldspathic rock. Decomposition of rock is continuous; so is the supply of clay. Clay also has been moved by glaciers, wind, and water from its original sources.

Even in its most simple form, making pottery requires five distinct

Frafra women in Bolgatanga, Ghana, pound dry clay lumps into a fine powder.

processes: digging the clay, preparing it, creating the form, drying the form, and firing it. Except in schools and demonstration centers, making clay forms is very much the same today as it has been in prehistoric times.

Preparation of Clay

No clay is usable immediately after being dug up, although clay that has been dredged from the banks of rivers, lakes, or ponds may be prepared for forming straightaway. But clay dug from deeper ground deposits usually takes a bit more preparation. Usually, clay has to be worked into a homogeneous mass, after lumps and extraneous matter have been removed. Sometimes clay is soaked in troughs, and the waste that rises to the top poured off. Most of the clay used in Africa is terra-cotta—a low-fire clay rich in iron.

It is not uncommon to see clay spread out on the ground or in shallow troughs and exposed to weather. Weathering breaks down small lumps and ages the clay. (Clay's malleability improves with aging.) The preparation is then helped by pommeling or treading it underfoot and then wedging it by hand through pounding, thumping, and rolling the clay. Some groups, as in northern Ghana (near Bolgatonga), dry the clay, then pound it with a stick into a fine powder, before mixing and kneading it with water.

Clay's plasticity and workability vary widely. Some clays are good for one process and not for another. Clays that are "greasy" are prepared by mixing them with a bit of sand or finely crushed shards (grog—which is fired clay); or the more sticky clays can be mixed with others that are less greasy or more sandy.

Forming

After clay is kneaded and prepared it is ready for forming. Here is where the process varies. Tools and equipment are very rudimentary, but the forms are perfect, functional, and beautiful. In some areas a simple wheel is used for forming, namely a board loosely mounted over a polished stone. In a town ten miles west of Accra, Weija, Ghana, every woman in the village makes pots. This is where they use a rudi-

mentary wheel and hollow out the clay from a lump, working from
the *bottom up*. A coil form is used later on just to modify the contours.
Corncobs, bits of wet leather, and stones are employed to supplement
versatile, skillful fingers. Yet, about a hundred miles to the north of
Weija, Ghana, in a town called Pankronu near Kumasi, Ashanti, women
work from the top down creating pots in two halves while walking back-
ward around the lump of clay. Body stiff-kneed, bent in half, she rotates
around the clay, which is on the ground, and the entire pot is hollowed
out and dragged up from a lump. There is no use of a wheel here.

After building up a form, these Ashanti women build a domelike bottom over a leather-hard top by patting flat cakes of clay and attaching
them bit by bit over the top. Finishing is completed using a bamboo
ring as a scraper and then bits of wet fabric, corncobs, and polished
stones to smooth the surface.

Pots, after being formed, are allowed to dry in open air under the
shade of trees, under roofs in some areas, under leaves or under larger
pots turned upside down. And in hot climates where the clay has been
well weathered and is full of organic and mineral fillers, it is dried directly in the sun.

Clay-working tools of Naomi, a Ga of Weija, Ghana. Old treasured stones,
smooth with work, corncobs, a pot containing water, rags, and a board
mounted over a rock that acts as a potter's wheel.

Naomi has been throwing pots for sixty years. Here she is centering a well-worked
ball of clay on her wheel.

While rotating the wheel with one hand, a thumb forces the first impression into the center of the clay.

The Ga work pots from the bottom up. Here she is forcing the clay up with four fingers of one hand while her other hand counteracts the pressure against the wall of the pot.

She continues to thin out the walls and shape them as she rotates the pot.

A closer view of Naomi's hands at work. Every once in a while she dips her hands into water to keep the clay moist and workable.

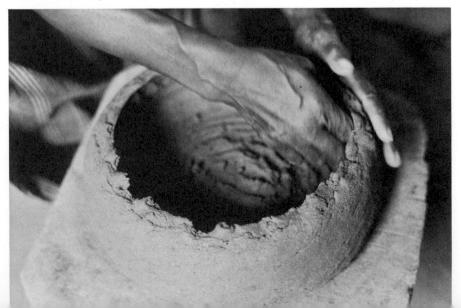

A corncob is used to smooth and even the thickness of the pot's walls.

The edge is shaped . . .

. . . with thumb and forefinger.

A wet cloth is used to apply finishing touches to edges.

A coil of clay is rolled out between her hands and attached to the belly of the pot.

Then, it is rubbed to join it to the existing wall . . .

. . . and smoothed with a stone that functions as a template.

A wet cloth provides a finishing touch.

Two versions on the same theme. Pots by Naomi of Weija.

Drying

Drying is necessary, otherwise when fired, steam would form in the walls of the pot and cause it to burst. When pottery is dry it is called greenware.

Firing

The firing of pots such as these, south of the Sahara, is usually in bonfires. Pots are stacked in different ways, then sticks or brush are

Every woman in Weija makes pots. This lady has been at the job for seventy-five years. Here she is stacking branches around a mound of dried pots in preparation for firing. A piece of sheet metal is then placed on top.

After about forty-five minutes to an hour of firing, the terra-cotta pots are lifted carefully out of the heap with aid of a long stick and placed on wood chips.

The hot pot causes the wood chips to smolder. The smoke helps color and seal the pot. When this is complete, the pots are placed in a shady area to cool.

piled over and around the pots and set on fire. Once lighted, the temperature rises rapidly reaching a maximum quickly, and thereafter the temperature falls slowly. In the Congo, pots are placed in a shallow pit, with an air passage at the sides, before it is covered with brush and lighted. Firing can take fifteen minutes to about two hours.

The result of this one and only firing of the clay is biscuit ware, a rather permeable body. (If a glaze is used for decoration, and it is rare, it is usually applied to the clay when it is in a green state.) There are always uncertainties in the firing process (a clay form does shrink in the drying and firing processes), but Naomi of Weija has been doing it for nearly sixty years, and her friend is still firing pots at seventy-five; so casualness is really expertise practiced and simplified.

After firing, pots are removed from the dying bonfire with long branches and one by one placed on the ground to cool. Some pots are treated for porosity and the system may vary. In Weija, they place some hot pots onto wood chips that quickly smoke, blackening the pot and reducing porosity somewhat. Other pots are put on the earth just to cool. Other groups use plant juice, palm oil, and still others apply resinous gum while the pot is still hot. Sometimes the women, as in Korhogo, Ivory Coast, rub and burnish the pot until a high polish is achieved.

On dry flat ground, on cloth, this Ashanti potter from Pankronu near Kumasi, Ghana, prepared a piece of clay. The Ashanti and Shai, unlike the Ga, who live no more than ninety miles or so away, start their pots from the top down, while standing up and bending over the pot. They do not use a wheel.

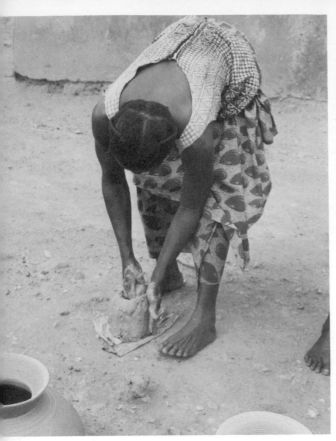
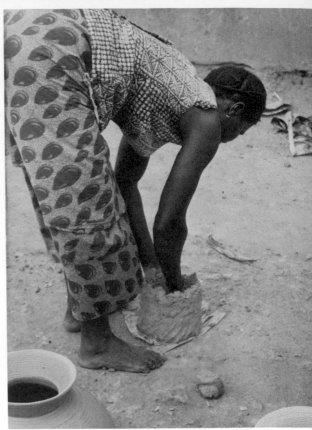

The clay is shaped into a mound and the hollowing-out process begins, while the potter circles around the pot.

Then, the lip is extended while drawing up excess clay from the side walls. Every once in a while, a bit of water is sprinkled over the clay pot.

A smooth stone is used as a template to apply the final finishing touches to the pot.

Top halves are drying in full sun.

Meanwhile, a top half that is leather-hard is turned top-to-the-ground and the cloth is pulled off.

Excess clay is scooped out and a ring made of bamboo is selected from an array of rings.

The ring carves away excess clay, thinning the top edge of the wall.

The interior is smoothed and evened out with a damp rag.

Flat pancakes of clay are patted and shaped . . .

. . . then attached to the wall, building the pot bottom into a dome shape.

The operation continues with more clay, quickly and deftly attached as her hands rotate around the pot . . .

. . . until the pot is almost completely formed, leaving only a fist-sized hole.

In the remaining opening, a corncob is used to smooth the outside, while a hand exerts opposite supporting pressure on the inside.

A bamboo ring is used to even out the thickness of the walls and smooth the interior, by feeling the thickness.

The remaining hole is covered over . . .

. . . and worked flat.

A corncob provides the final texturing. In large pots, a rough exterior makes a pot easier to hold than a smooth, potentially slippery surface.

Decorating

Pots usually have some kind of surface decoration that has a functional purpose. A ceramic piece with a raised design or a design-roughened area is easier to carry, and is less apt to slip out of wet hands. Designs usually are made by modeling clay embellishments and attaching them to the pot while the clay is moist or by incising designs in leather-hard clay; by impressing wet clay with pointed sticks or rough materials such as braids of straw; by applying coils, lumps, or braids of clay when wet; by burnishing and polishing it; and more rarely now by painting designs using brush or knife with mixtures of earth colors such as kaolin and ocher with water or peanut oil.

When the pot goes to market, it sells just for a few cents, but may take a purchaser a half hour to select—turning, handling it, and studying a pot's features before deciding.

Today virtually all religious pottery has disappeared, except for a few clay fetish sculptures. But women are still the potters, often in parallel status to the blacksmith. There are exceptions. Ashanti women are forbidden to incorporate any anthropomorphic or zoomorphic decorations, as mentioned earlier. Men, though, are learning the ceramists' arts in trade schools. Exceptions are less rare today.

The ground is prepared for firing with a thin layer of wood-ash, to keep the ground dry. Courtesy: Mr. John Francis and Mr. J. K. Amoah

Pots are arranged in layers and more firewood is leaned closely against the pots. *Courtesy: Mr. John Francis and Mr. J. K. Amoah*

The woman sets fire to the wood. *Courtesy: Mr. John Francis and Mr. J. K. Amoah*

The firewood starts to burn. *Courtesy: Mr. John Francis and Mr. J. K. Amoah*

Pots are eventually left in glowing coals. The final stage is reached. *Courtesy: Mr. John Francis and Mr. J. K. Amoah*

The fired pots ready for market.

Some Shai pots from the Dodowa area of Ghana.

TRY IT

One can make excellent pots with no expenditure of money. Search for clay sources—often along the bank of a stream. If there are rocks and debris, sift the clay through a screen. Prepare the clay by grinding and pounding it as with a mortar and pestle or by soaking and stirring it several times; letting it settle and pouring off impurities. Allow clay to age in a barrel for weeks. If the clay is too sticky, add powdered, fired clay (grog) to the mixture until it is workable, or try some sand. Also, try mixing different clays, sticky, greasy, sandy, crumbly kinds until you achieve the proper consistency. Then take out a lump. Knead it, roll it, slap piece on piece, and press out air bubbles. Shape your form. Use stones, corncobs, and bits of wet leather to smooth and shape your piece. Decorate it with coils, impressions, or incisions. Allow it to dry slowly and completely in a shady, open air spot. Then when you have formed several pieces of green-ware, build a bonfire kiln the same way as described in the illustrations. Take care not to break your pots when removing them with a long stick. Low fire clays, such as the terra-cottas of Africa, are fragile and porous. It may be better to allow your work to cool before unstacking the pieces. Your challenge is to create a simple, functional, symmetrical form—aided only by eye and hand. It takes practice.

These pots, from Nigeria, are more pointed at the base.

Pots and calabashes stack well when they have rounded bottoms. The round form is generally stronger. Note the incised designs on these pots from Bolgatanga, Ghana.

Ceremonial lidded bowl. Yoruba, Nigeria.

A potter from Korhogo burnishes completed pots with stones and beads outside . . .

. . . and inside.

Textures vary and are determined in part by the function and size of the pot.

A large ceramic pot by a Watussi of Burundi. *Courtesy: Smithsonian Institution*

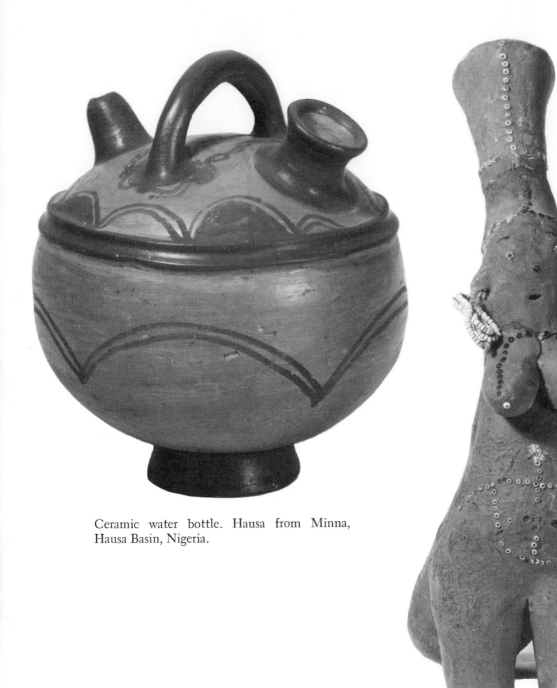

Ceramic water bottle. Hausa from Minna,
Hausa Basin, Nigeria.

Ceramic figure of a woman. Zulu, Natal, South
Africa. *Courtesy: Smithsonian Institution*

3

ʌʌʌʌʌʌʌʌʌʌʌʌ

AFRICAN
TEXTILE
ARTS

ʌʌʌʌʌʌʌʌʌʌʌʌ

BACKGROUND

There is evidence that textiles were produced south of the Sahara well before European contacts. Archaeologists found that bast, a bundled fiber from bark or stalks and flat grass, such as flax, raffia, hemp, was woven at Igbo-Ukwu in Nigeria. Although no trace of cotton was found, bast cloth, like cotton, had selvages that indicate a weaving process, probably on a loom. Later in the thirteenth century there is evidence that cotton was utilized in Benin, Nigeria.

Beaten bark cloth also was a popular textile over much of the sub-continent. Since it may be cut, sewn, embroidered, appliquéd and painted, it was a useful material. But it is quite fragile when wet, and stronger fabrics such as cotton, when available, tend to replace bark cloth. Bast textiles, such as woven raffia, beaten bark cloth, and cotton, made up the most important group of materials. Wool was, and is, rarely

59

Beaten bark cloth was a popular textile over much of the subcontinent. This bark cloth carpet is from the Haya tribe. Bukova district, Tanzania.

used, except in the Sudan; silk, which is not native to Africa, was brought in by the Dutch in the seventeenth century.

There are two basic types of looms used in weaving. One type is a fixed frame vertical loom (see diagram page 109), a form now used mainly by women that dates back to Egypt in 2500 B.C. (also was used by the ancient Greeks and is very similar to a Navaho loom). It consists of two wooden posts anchored into the ground and connected with a crossbar at the top. Warp threads are tied to the top beam with their loose ends weighted down by small stones or balls of hardened clay. The width was anywhere from 20 to 46 inches. Weaving was accomplished from the top down. Modified versions of this loom are still used today.

The other type of loom is a double heddle (see diagram on page 116), narrow-band (4 to 6 inches), horizontal treadle loom, which is used only by men. These looms can be rolled up and easily carried by itinerant weavers from village to village. Men weave as a vocation. But women, using the fixed loom, weave as an avocation—making cloth for their children's wrappers and for themselves. Only in the Congo, men use the vertical loom for making raffia cloth. It may well be that in earlier times the vertical loom was used by men, up to the time that the strip loom was introduced. Women are the spinners; they prepare cotton by cleaning and spinning the raw material into a well-twisted thread. About fifty years ago, King Nachoya, a leader of the Bamum, had 1,300 looms in operation and the king himself designed new patterns. Although the market for handweaving is considerably smaller now, there still is a demand for handwoven fabrics.

The variety of textile designs is enormous, considering the limitations in size and the kinds of weaving looms and in the range of raw materials. Indigo (blue), perhaps the world's oldest and most important dyestuff for 4,000 years (native source: India), and white are indigenous colors all over Africa. In some cases, yarn was predyed and then woven into striped patterns; in other instances the entire fabric was dyed. These narrow-band fabrics were then stitched together into wider yard goods. White fabrics also were decorated by stamping, a direct-printing technique that utilized carved pieces of calabash or other materials; resist methods whereby fabric is tied into bunches, or seeds and nuts are sewn or tied (tied-and-dyed) into fabric with raffia before dipping in dye. Another resist was used, a cassava paste, and, more recently, wax in a batik process to create patterns before dyeing. Fabric was also painted, and a corroding method was used to bleach away patterns in dark-dyed cloth.

Over the years, each design had intrinsic value and its own meaning. The symbolic use of patterns was widespread. A zigzag might suggest lightning, snakes, water, fire, or the mane of an antelope. A circled dot often refers to the sun as a source of great vitality.

Kuba kings swathed themselves in a vast accumulation of status symbols beginning with an embroidered kilt, thirty feet long, made of tiny patchworks of beaten bark cloth with edging of raffia velvet, geometric lace, and tassels; the shirt was a mesh of cowrie shells; other adornment on feet, arms, head, and neck made for an inscrutable, immovable power. Most divine kings of Africa displayed themselves ceremoniously in that way.

Kuba kings swathed themselves in a vast accumulation of status symbols such as this kilt, sometimes thirty feet long, made of tiny patchworks of beaten bark cloth.

The Ashanti kings had their own Kente cloth patterns, which they wore in an elegant toga style over one shoulder. If anyone else wore that pattern they would be put to death. This was royal property. The weaving of Kente cloth was said to have been started in the seventeenth century, using the indigenous indigo and white on cotton grown and spun locally. When the Dutch introduced silk cloth, Gold Coast women patiently unraveled the silk and weavers reused it in their Kente cloth. Legend has it that the first weaver was a big black-and-yellow spider spinning its web and that this inspired the Ashanti weavers.

The center of Kente weaving was in Bonwire, Ashanti, Ghana. It was the custom, then, for all designs to be shown to the king of the Ashantis. Designs he liked were reserved for his exclusive use. Others he allocated among his royal court or bestowed on great men in the kingdom. Each family or clan had its exclusive Kente design. The clan, social status, or sex of wearers was represented by patterns that had their own names such as *Mmeda*—"It has never come before," or *Abusa ye dom*—"If you have a crown you have people who fight for you." Colors of Kente cloth were more subtle when they were made of silk, but silk is not available today. Cotton and rayons are much brighter and to the contemporary Ashanti's preference.

Ashanti (and Mangbetu) stamped patterns onto fabric for adinkra designed mourning garments. Each imprint communicated a symbolic significance. Resist techniques were used in the Cameroons and Nigeria. Baulé tribesmen folded cloth and tied it around seeds, stones, and sticks with raffia before dyeing it—usually with indigo. In Oshogbo, Nigeria, adire cloth was made. It is a Yoruba word for "tie and dye." Cassava paste applied with feather or straw was drawn into intricate designs, each one unique. Today, fabric designs of Africans respond to fashion whims just as fashion does in Paris. Cloth pieces are datable. Some women would not be seen wearing last year's pattern.

Plangi, a tie and dye technique, is found in all of West Africa from Nigeria to western Sudan. In Mali and the northern Ivory Coast (near Korhogo) a cloth is painted into patterns that have fetish significance. In Mali, patterns are drawn with alkaline soap and then the fabric is dipped into a mud bath. The Senufos (and Bambaras) use a leaf as dye for the first drawing and then trace over it with a mud material that acts as a mordant and turns the original green dye color black. These fabrics once were used as hunting costumes.

In the Kasai and Kiwilu territories in central Congo, plushlike raffia is woven and knotted into various patterns. This, too, is prestige cloth as the Kente and the women's cloth of Nigeria, Akwete (Iboland), and Okene (north of Benin). Cloths of fine raffia and raffia and cotton, as well, are woven today—in Dahomey, Nigeria, and the Cameroons, and in the Kasai area of the Republic of Zaïre. Among the Kubas, this fine raffia cloth is produced by teams of men and women. The women embroider designs on the mats that men weave.

Appliqué was a commonly known technique used in patching up holes in textiles. But appliqué is also deliberate in the symbolic brilliantly colored hangings of Dahomey.

Kente cloth called *Sika futuru*, meaning gold dust. The size is longer and almost as wide as a bedspread for a double bed.

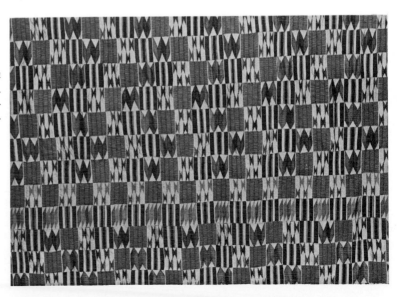

The Ashanti kings had their own Kente cloth that they wore, toga style, over one shoulder. This is a Kente two-harness loom.

A strip of Kente cloth more than seventy years old made of silk called *Mmeda*, "It has never come before."

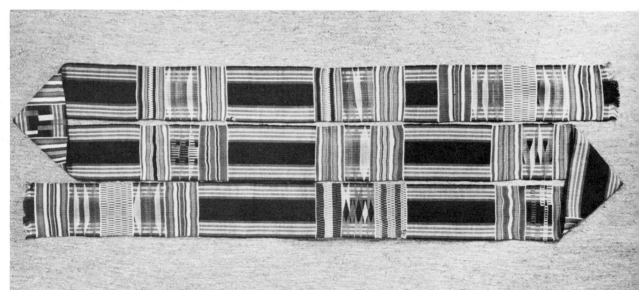

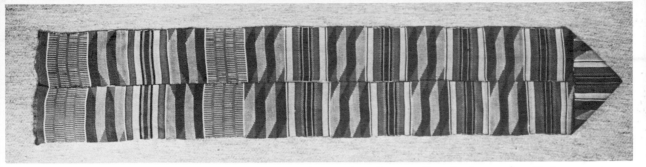

A variation of gold dust, this time with a blue rather than a saffron background, called *Abusa ye dom*, "If you have a crown you have people who will fight for you."

A white silk Kente strip called *Aberewa ben*, "He is omnipotent."

A modern-day use of the Kente design as a place mat. Fibers for Kente cloth have run the gamut from *Kyen Kyen* tree fibers for the first Kente cloth, to unraveled silk, cotton, and rayon, to this all-cotton version.

/\/\/\/\/\/\/\/\/\/\/\/\/\

PART ONE

Decorating Fabrics

RESIST PROCESSES

Resist is a process that protects areas of a fabric from the penetration of dyes. One property a resist must have is not to dissolve in the dye bath, yet be removable after dyeing. Two of several resist techniques are the making of plangi and adire cloth.

Preparing Indigo Dye

Indigo manufacturing, once *indicum* (ink) of the Romans, required the gathering of dew-covered young leaves of the *elu* plant, called *tinto* by some. The leaves were well pounded in deep wooden mortars so that rolls or balls as big as a fist could be formed. Then these balls were exposed to the sun for several days to dry. After that they were pounded again and placed into a pot that had a hole in the bottom to allow for seepage. This pot sat in a larger vat. The pot was filled with wood ashes made from burning the wood of the same bush. Spring water was poured over the ashes. Little by little the water seeped through into the underpot. The process was repeated over and over again, then the pot containing the indigo liquor was placed in the sun for ten days until a thick cream skin formed. This was skimmed off and saved. The rest was discarded. The resulting solution is called *indican*.

The process is so complex that it is no wonder that a synthetic indigo is now used producing comparable results with half the effort. Dyers now mix one teaspoon of indigo grains (60 percent) with a bit of warm water to dissolve it. Then a half teaspoon of caustic soda flakes and half a teaspoon of sodium hydrosulphite are dissolved in cold water and this is added to two pints of warm water. Next, one and one-half teaspoons of salt dissolved in a small amount of warm water is carefully added to the indigo solution. The mixture is stirred gently for a few minutes using a glass rod or wooden stick and is allowed to stand in the vat until it has become a dark yellowish green color. Fabric is now added to the dye, and after ten minutes, the fabric is pulled out to allow it to oxidize in the air. (It turns blue.) If a more intense color is desired, the fabric is returned to the dye, repeating the process until the desired intensity has been achieved. The textile is allowed to dry. If one buys it and wants the color not to come off on one's body—Africans love blue-tinted skin—then it has to be treated by washing it with acetic acid, or vinegar, and warm soapy water. Vinegar helps set the dye. Then unfold the cloth and spread a cup of detergent and half a cup of regular salt on the cloth and cover it with warm water. Swish the cloth around in the water until the salt and soap are dissolved, and allow it to remain this way, undisturbed for at least three days. Then rinse it well in clear water several times before drying it. Use large ceramic vats for dyeing the cloth.

This is indigo before pounding and preparation.

Indigo vats made of terra-cotta are mounted in adobe.

Fabric is dipped in and out of the dye.

The textile is left on a wooden board to oxidize in the air.

Then it is returned to the vat.

Adire Eleso

Adire Eleso (eleso means "small stones" or "seeds") is similar to plangi, or tie-dye, in which a design is created by pleating, folding, or twisting the material, sewing or tying it in place with raffia and then dyeing it in indigo vats. After the cloth is dry, the stitching is removed, exposing the design that was protected by folding, twisting, and sewing. The cloth is sometimes redipped so that contrast in the pattern is not too great. Sometimes cottonseeds or nuts are placed in the cloth and then stitched in place, particularly to reserve with resist the shape of a small circle.

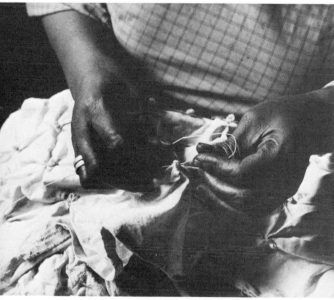

This is adire eleso, similar to plangi, or tie dye. Raffia thread is wrapped around small gathers in the cotton.

It is tied tightly to keep dye from seeping under it.

After dyeing it is allowed to dry.

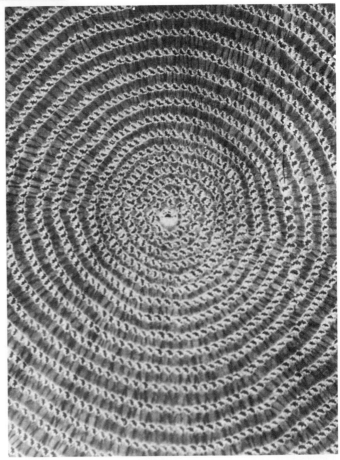

Indigo dyed tie dye from Oshogbo, Nigeria.

The design, which is formed by sewing, is ready to be pulled apart by giving the fabric a good hard yank. Each line is pulled apart this way.

This is the fabric after being pulled apart. Lines formed by stitches are evident.

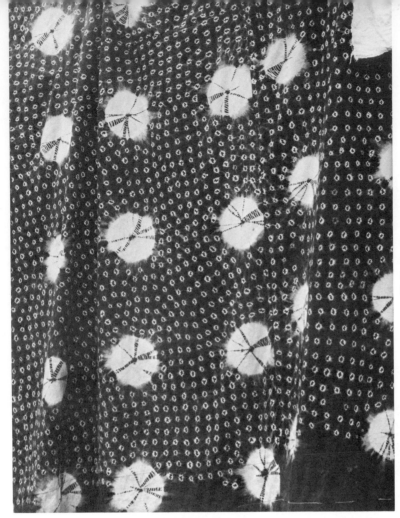

Use of two sizes of circles—the larger circle was folded and the smaller one puckered.

A variation of *adire eleso*.

Adire Eleko

In *adire eleko*, the design is painted on cloth with a starch made from cassava flour called *lafun*. The starch is boiled with blue and white alum to prevent it from dissolving in the dye vat. Sometimes the cassava designs are applied with the rib of a palm frond (looks like a piece of straw) or with a feather. Other times the men cut a stencil from zinc. The stencil is placed on the material and starch is spread over it with cardboard, wood, or metal. Then the stencil is lifted off and placed on the next spot to repeat the design. The starch is allowed to dry before dyeing. After the dyeing process, the starch is flaked off the cloth and the fabric is redipped so that contrast is reduced, as in tie-dye.

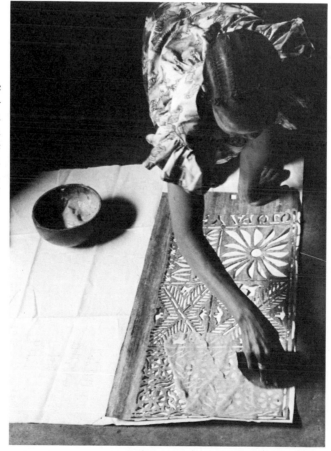

Adire eleko is the application of cassava paste as a starch resist. In this case, the craftsman from Oshogbo, Nigeria, is applying it over a zinc stencil.

She then gingerly peels off the stencil, which is stiff but flexible . . .

. . . leaving a moist pattern of cassava paste, which then has to dry before dyeing in indigo.

Here she is applying cassava paste with a piece of palm frond to create another effect over a woven striped fabric.

After dyeing, the *adire eleko* fabrics are left to dry on a line . . .

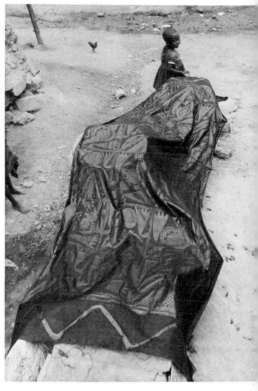

. . . or over some boards.

After drying, the cassava is washed away.

The fabric is ready to wear. Note her beautiful textiles. This probably is this year's design from Oshogbo, Nigeria.

A pattern made by drawing palm fronds charged with cassava paste across the fabric.

A close-up.

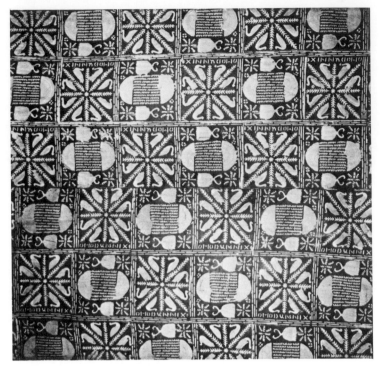

Another stencil pattern.

TRY IT

A simple paste resist can be made with three tablespoons (wheat) flour, one-half teaspoon alum, one cup of cold water placed in the top of a double boiler. It needs to be cooked and stirred continuously until it becomes semitransparent.

Another variation is to add one tablespoon of laundry starch to the mixture.

Use any fabric dye that is a specific for the fabric being used. Check to see whether any mordant is needed to fix the dye and make it colorfast. Use a brush instead of straw if you like and heavy duty aluminum foil for a stencil.

⋀⋀⋀
PRINTING PROCESS—ADINKRA

Adinkra cloth was originally used as a cloth to wrap around one when in mourning. But now it has other uses; when backgrounds are colorful, it can be used as curtains, bedspreads, and so on. The cloth is not washable until it has set for one to two years—yes, years.

Badee bark is peeled from the tree and soaked overnight in water. It is pounded and boiled again in the same water. Large tins are used. Each day (not night) the liquor is boiled in the same water for a week. In the last few days an iron ore stone is placed in the drum to give the dye its black color. One half-gallon is left from an original five-gallon tin. When cool, the white of an egg is added to the dyestuff to give it the characteristic glossy effect of adinkra.

Calabashes are carved, to allow for raised areas that will print as a positive. Negative areas are cut away. A tripod arrangement of splinters (they look like applicator sticks) are tied to the stamp. The fabric is stretched tautly over a level, horizontal wooden board that is covered with a padding of burlap. The calabash stamp is dipped into the dye; excess is shaken off and then the stamp is pressed onto the fabric.

Sometimes a wooden comb is used to draw lines and borders around areas. Repeating is optional. Different stamps are often used on the same fabric. After printing, the fabric is allowed to dry in the sun.

There are two types of *adinkra*—plain and embroidered (*nwomu*), where strips of fabric are attached by hand stitching, or by embroidery with bright, primary colors.

As mentioned earlier, this fabric is not washable until it has been exposed to light and air for at least a year. The original mourning cloth consisted of black glossy *adinkra* designs (each with its symbolic meaning) printed on black cotton. The wearer actually wore a clothing poster that transmitted a message.

While nursing her baby, this lady from Ntonsu near Kumasi, Ghana, is peeling badee bark and throwing it into a barrel where it will soak in water overnight.

The bark is cooking in the same water until the water is reduced by half in these five-gallon tins.

In the last stage, it will further cook with an iron-ore stone, which acts as a mordant and will turn the dye black. Note that she is working—lifting the hot, heavy gallons—while carrying a baby on her back.

Yardage is emboidered together with a satin blanket stitch.

The fabric does not overlap but butts together. This stitch sews the two pieces together by going under one piece and over another in a figure-eight pattern. Every once in a while the color will be changed.

A pot full of carved calabashes, ready for stamping. Each design has its symbolic meaning.

Calabash stamps ready for action—on the left, aya (the fern), which means "I am not afraid of you," a symbol of defiance.

Fabric is stretched and tacked on a board that has a straw mat liner.

A comb shape is dipped in dye and drawn across the fabric . . .

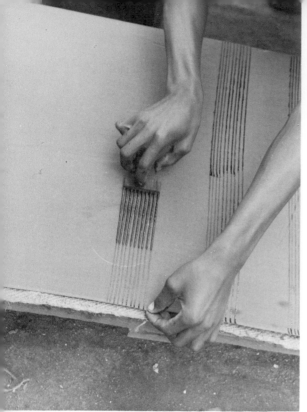

. . . as shown in this detail. This pattern is called *Nhwimu*, meaning "crossing."

Then another stamp is dipped into dye, excess is shaken off and then . . .

. . . the stamp is pressed onto the fabric. This pattern is called *aban* for fence, representing fenced homes, a protector, or a symbol meaning safe and sound.

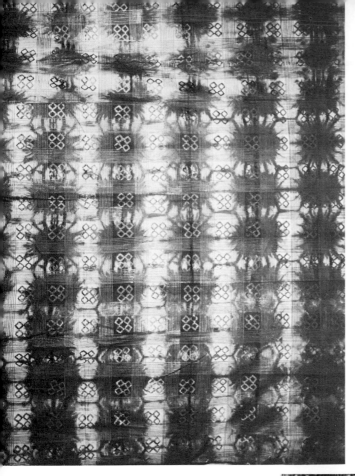

An *adinkra* pattern on a dip-dyed fabric. Colors are black on gold. The *adinkra* dye is a glossy black which helps to contrast with the matte black of the background.

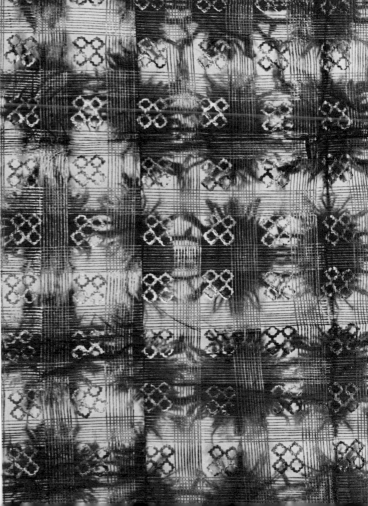

A close-up of a Ntonsu *adinkra* textile. The fabric more than covers a double bed.

Adinkra mourning cloth, glossy black on black fabric.

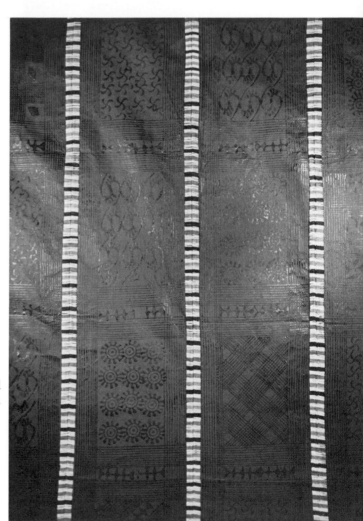

Another fabric with embroidery and different *adinkra* patterns in each rectangle.

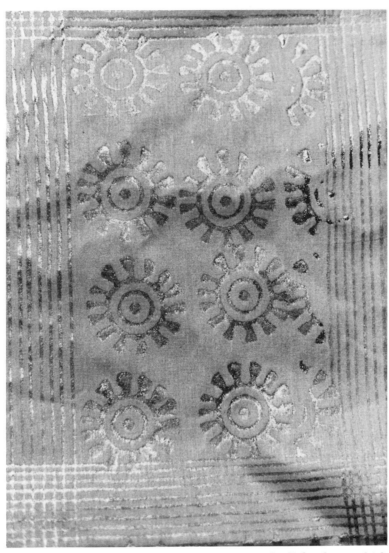

A close-up of one box, the pattern is a version of *adinkra hene*, which is chief of all designs, and forms the basis for *adinkra* printing.

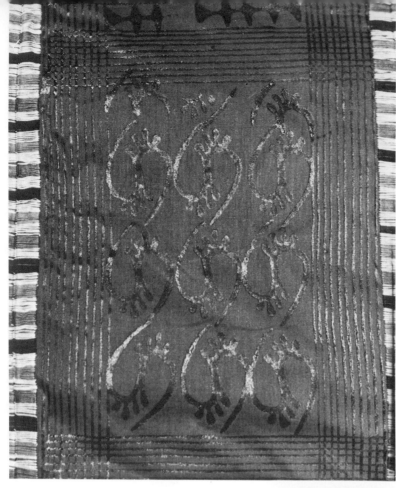

Another design called *bin-ka-bi*, meaning "avoid conflicts." It is a symbol of unity.

And still another of at least ten different patterns. Colors are black on emerald green with yellow, red, and green embroidery. This design represents the talons of an eagle. This is also said to be shaved on the heads of some court attendants.

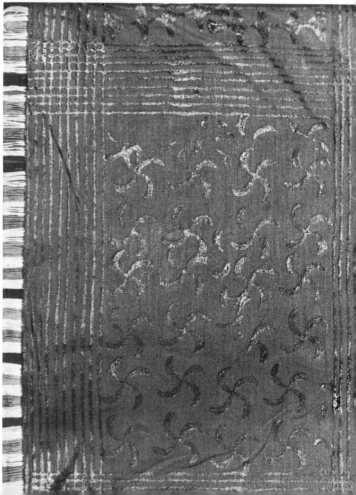

TRY IT

A more permanent, washable paint can be used. Try acrylic (polymer) paint, the kind used for "oil" paintings. After drying completely, it should be washable. Prang has an acrylic textile medium that works beautifully, too. Brush or roll paint onto your block and print by stamping it on your clean cloth. Make certain there is a padding of newspaper under your cloth. This makes for a better impression.

Instead of using a carved calabash, try carving balsa wood, basswood, or even expanded urethane (foam).

PAINTING ON COTTON CLOTH— SENUFO STYLE

Dance and hunting clothing was decorated with a kind of symbolic painting. The painting had mystical properties because it played a part in the poro-cult of secret societies. Cotton cloth on which the design is painted is made of home-cleaned, spun, woven natural white cotton strips, four inches wide, sewn together into various-sized cloth. The material is absorbent and keeps the runny dye from spreading. Figures of birds, snakes, fish, crocodiles, turtles, and poro-figures represented as masked dancers and fetishes are scattered randomly along with suns, triangles, and circular ornaments. The figures are meant to bring luck to the hunter and to protect him. Indeed, when seen against its background, the spirit blends in with the foliage and appears to camouflage the wearer.

After stretching and nailing a piece of washed cotton (now dry) tautly on a flat wooden board, without any predrawing, the artist dips his dull-bladed knife into a boiled dye made from green leaves and draws the outline. Some large areas may be filled in with an old toothbrush or small nail brush.

The leaves and stem of the falma bush are boiled to get a yellowish green dye. After this dye has been applied, a second coating of dye is added directly over the yellow green layer, in the same way, with knife and tooth or hand brush. This second material is made from sludgy decayed mud dug from between roots of trees in swampy areas. The sludge is filtered and stirred into a thin solution by adding water. In the clay pot it appears black, but is actually transparent when one dips a finger into it. Apparently, it contains fermenting agents and iron-bearing (iron sulfate) substances that induce a chemical reaction when combined with the yellow green leaf dye, causing the dye to turn black. This "mud" dye probably is mordant, keeping the color from bleaching in the sun and providing some washability.

Leaves and stems of the falma bush are boiled to get a yellowish green, almost sepia colored, dye.

Handwoven cotton fabric, with four-inch widths that have been hand-sewn together, is tacked and stretched on a board.

With a dull-bladed knife, the Senufo craftsman dips it into the yellow green dye and applies it with sure-handed lines to the fabric . . .

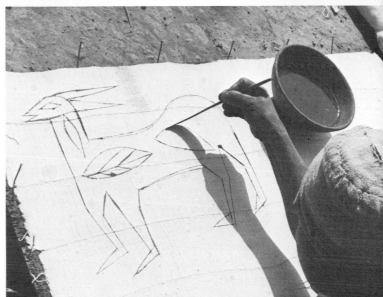

. . . until the entire outline is completed, as well as definition of details.

Then broader areas are filled
in with a toothbrush charged
with the same dye.

When the first application of yellow green dye has dried, a second application is made
directly over the first . . .

. . . with an iron-bearing material made from decayed mud. This acts as a mordant.

These textiles are from Fakaha, Ivory Coast, near Korhogo.

Figures have mystical properties that play a part in secret societies.

Different artists have styles, symbols, and arrangements that are unique to them.

Poro figures, animals, and birds suggest a hunt.

Once worn as clothing, pieces now become magnificent wall decorations.

A scene from the village of Fakaha Ivory Coast.

TRY IT

Try painting with a dull, curve-bladed knife, a cotton swab, tongue depressor, toothbrush—any instrument. For dye, use an acrylic textile paint diluted somewhat so that it will flow without running out of control. The texture of your cloth should be absorbent. Wash out fillers before painting on the cloth.

⋏⋏⋏
APPLIQUÉ

An appliqué of large bright figures bearing mystical symbolism creates a dramatic effect as a wall hanging. This type of cloth mural was originally created for the king, who was a powerful figure controlling a mighty army in which there was a tribe of Amazons.

Working at the court were smiths, wood-carvers, gold- and silver-casters, weavers and embroiderers who made wall hangings, furniture, cushions, clothing, jewelry, parasols, tents—using their craft to embellish the divine king and his surroundings.

The symbols used in this work were a language that everyone understood. Appliqué came later and evolved as a simpler form than the original weaving of symbols in cloth. Most of the stories told were of wartime exploits, complete with decapitations, hangings, etc.

The stories live on in these symbols, although today the art form is not as inspired as it once was. (Tourists are creating a great demand for these pieces.) Each king had his stories and commensurate symbols. Agadja (1708–1728) is depicted by a coat of arms and a ship. It was during this reign that Dahomey had the first contact with Europe and Catholicism. Agonglo (1789–1797) is described with a coat of arms and a pineapple. Agonglo literally means that lightning strikes the palm tree but is powerless against the pineapple. Legend has it that the king was standing under a palm tree taking shelter from a storm. The tree was struck by lightning, but the king escaped. He compared himself to the pineapple, which, according to their mythology, is never struck by lightning.

Lions, sharks, eggs, brooms, stones, a foot, buffalo, sparrow, gun, jars of indigo—are all part of the picture story told in appliqué as a creative history book.

Processwise, the technique is quite usual and universal. Forms of brightly colored cotton are cut from cloth, basted in place on the background, which is usually black cotton, and then attached along folded back edges with a blind hemming stitch. Embroidery fills in the details, such the pattern on a pineapple, the feathers of a bird. Very simple stitches are used, such as the running stitch and outline stitch.

Abomey is the center in Dahomey for creating these bright appliqué hangings. Each figure symbolizes another meaning that has its roots in folklore and history.

Birds, pipes, weapons, dye pots, coats of arms—are among some of the symbols that read like visual history books.

Adadja, a king, is depicted by a coat of arms and a ship. Agonglo is described by a coat of arms and a pineapple. A broom, a stone and a foot represent Ago-li-agbo, the last king who was placed at the head of the kingdom by the French. Agoliagbo literally means "Be strong! Allada has tripped over a stone, but has not fallen down. Glory be to the French!" It seems almost every king is represented in this hanging.

This one from the Aizo region is of Dako, a local warrior (of about 1625) who lost a foot. It symbolizes a fierce battle. Note the cowrie shell ornaments around his one foot and neck. Jars of indigo are tied to his arms, legs, and mouthpiece. Dako, in one sense, is said to mean: "Dako kills and the jar of indigo rolls." Legend has it that one day Dako took by surprise his enemy Aizo, who was preparing indigo. Dako killed him and put his body in the jar and made it roll.

These cartoonlike symbols are illustrations of mythological legends. Where fact of history leaves off and fancy begins is a romantic guess.

In this appliqué, figures march across the fabric like a parade.

PART TWO

/\.\/\.\/\.\/\.\/\.\/\.\/\.\/\.\

Weaving

Considering the simple, basic equipment used, such as a fixed frame loom or a two-harness narrow strip loom, marvelous fabrics are woven. Some of the inventiveness and variety depends on the use of repeat designs and how strips of woven fabric are sewn together. Counterpoint in contrast and pattern is possible.

When asked why weavers don't use wider looms, we were told that strips sewn together have more body and therefore drape better than unstitched fabric. That may be so. Schools have been trying to introduce wider looms, but have not been too successful. When people want fabric with less body, they buy the cheaper imported machine-made fabric. Meanwhile, the handwoven variety has a beautiful texture, very rarely found in commercial weaving, and a ready market.

/\.\/\.\

PREPARING COTTON—CLEANING
AND SPINNING

Picked cotton must have seeds removed before spinning. Generally, seeds are rolled out with an iron rod rolling the cotton forward on a flat stone or board. Then the cotton is loosened and loosely wrapped spiral fashion around a distaff. By pulling away a few strands at the end, it is attached to a spindle consisting of a short rod and whorl mounted near the distal end. The fibers are attached at the proximal end of the spindle in a half-hitch (or in a notch) and the spindle is spun until the length of fibers is given a sufficient twist. This length is wrapped on the spindle and the process is repeated. The point of the weighted spindle sits on a rock, in a dish, or on a piece of metal, and is made to rotate. As the spindle rotates, it draws fibers out into a strand twisted into a uniform diameter. The operation is draw, stretch, and twist. Then cotton is twisted and wound on a spindle.

Picked cotton must have the seeds removed before spinning.

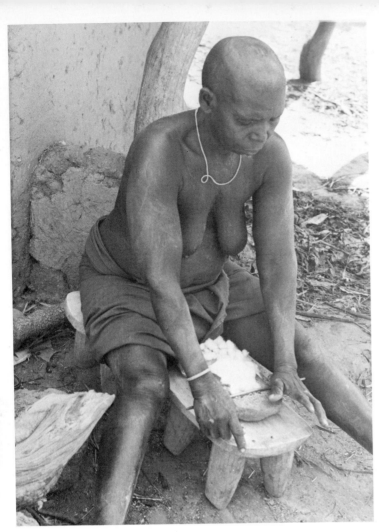

Generally, seeds are rolled out with an iron rod, rolling the cotton forward on a flat board or stone. The village is Fakaha, Ivory Coast.

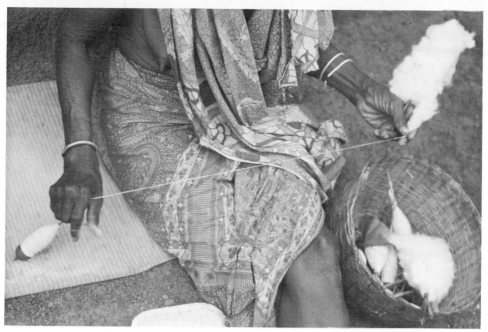

The cotton is loosened and loosely wrapped spiral-fashion around a distaff. The fibers are attached at the proximal end of the spindle in a half hitch, and the spindle is spun until the length of fibers is given a sufficient twist. (Also see photo at bottom of left page.)

WEAVING

Simple weaving is the interweaving of two sets of threads. Weft threads are woven through warp threads, which are stationary, foundation threads. Textile pattern and texture is achieved by the various ways a warp can be strung, such as different colors and members of warp threads, by the color and texture of the weft thread and how the weft is passed under and over the warp, such as using different counts. Changing colors of weft threads every few lines with a striped warp, for instance, creates a plaid; alternation of the numbers of warp threads crossed by the weft creates a pattern.

Woman's Loom

The woman's loom is vertical and stationary. The female weaver is not the itinerant who carries a loom on her back from village to village. Her needs are different and centered on domesticity—herself, home, and children. She weaves for those needs.

The woman's loom is vertical and stationary.

The woman's loom looks very much like a Navaho loom. The warp passes around upper and lower bars like a roller towel (producing twice the length) instead of being strung flat between the two bars. In order to alternate the warp, it is pulled forward by a heddle, which consists of two long flexible sticks with string loops fastened along it and around alternate warp threads. As the heddle stick is pulled, it raises (or lowers) one set of warp threads, making room for the passage of a shuttle. There may be additional heddles, which pull forward a particular pattern as for brocade weaving.

Brocade is a process of drawing extra design weft between the plain weave wefts. These extra different colors or textures float or skip over several warps at a time. Each layer of plain weave is woven as usual, beaten down well with the beater, a comblike reed tool that compacts uneven spaces. Wefts of different colors and textures are wound on long bobbin sticks (shuttles) and woven through the extra design warp to create the brocade pattern. The brocade design then predominates.

Two examples of woman's brocade weaves
called *okene* cloth, woven of silk in the
southeastern part of Nigeria. The colors are
gold on a dark blue background.

Raffia Weaving

Raffia is a native bast of Africa. Ribs of leaves of the raffia palm provide the soft, supple, yet tough fiber—raffia. There are two kinds of raffia—the white kind that comes in wide firm strands that are supple and tough and a cheaper yellowish kind that is not so supple and does not wear so well. Both raffias are used in a dry state.

The raffia loom, which essentially is the same as the woman's loom, permits the manufacture of small pieces of cloth, and mats with or without a selvage. Most raffia cloths are overlapped and sewn to form larger pieces. The edges then are hemmed.

The finished piece often is placed in a mortar with cold water and beaten with a smooth ivory pestle to make it more resilient. Appliqué is often used, particularly to cover worn areas.

Cut-pile cloths, the Kasai velvets, as mentioned earlier, are a prestige cloth. Designs are varied and can be very complex. A mat serves as a foundation that is then worked with needle and palm thread (raffia) into looped designs. A small sharp knife is used to clip out loops into tufts.

The raffia loom, which is essentially the same as the woman's loom, permits the weaving of small pieces of cloth and mats, with or without selvage. The origin of this loom is from the Congo.

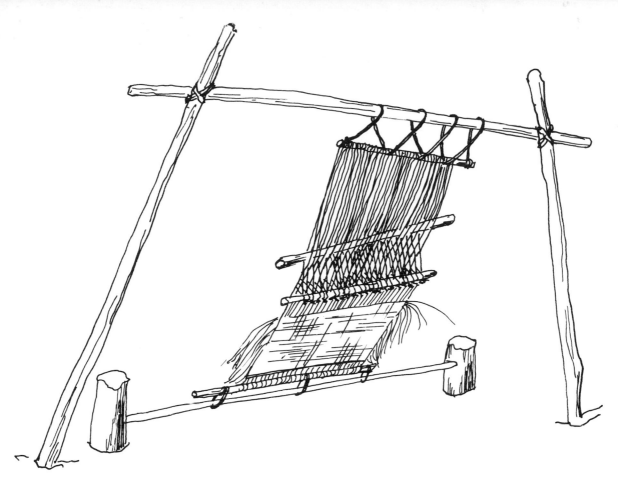

A drawing of the raffia loom as it looks mounted and ready for weaving.

Two raffia bags of the Bamileke people of Cameroon. These are used for hunting in the forest.

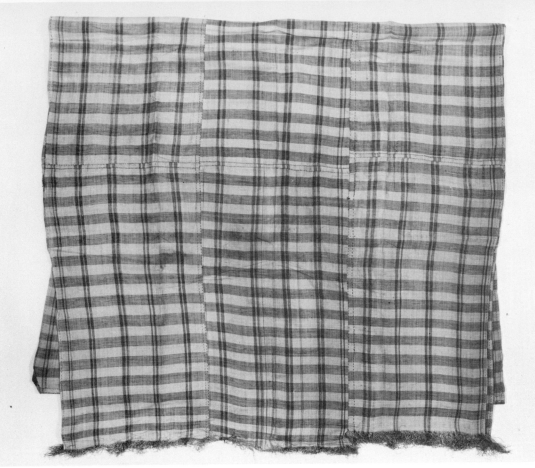

This raffia cloth garment was made from eighteen pieces sewed together. From Yaka, Congo.

Man's Loom

Weavings are often used as part of the bride price for a wife. The man's loom is often called a strip loom because the width from selvage to selvage is so narrow, four to six inches. This type of loom was used in Senegal since 1455—virtually unchanged. The warp, in a man's loom, is horizontal to the ground, fastened between a cloth bar and a weighted stone about sixty feet in front of the loom. This provides tension for the warp. Usually two heddles are hung from above on a pulley to control opposite sets of warp.

Among the Baulé, Guro, and Senufo are marvelous hand-carved pulleys taking their inspiration from myths, men, and animals, ceremonial masks, and the like. They have a mystical significance. A reed beater hung from above the loom battens each weft close together into an even line after weft is run through the shed (triangular space formed by opposite warp threads and the heddles held at extreme position).

Unlike women who weave, men weave as a vocation, often in co-operatives such as this one in Tamala, Ghana.

Implements for weaving are improvised home-made devices.

These two rods are used to string the warp (warping) so that a cross is formed between the rods forming the shed. The warp then can be transferred to lease sticks on the loom keeping alternate threads of the shed separate for stringing through heddles.

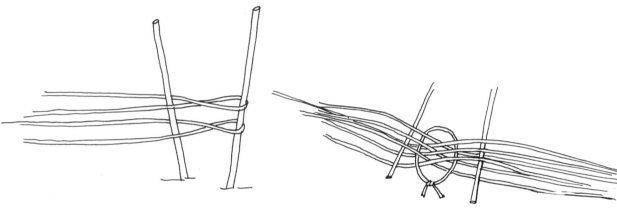

The left diagram describes the above photo. And the right figure shows how the cross is tied to keep the shed separated so that one can clearly distinguish alternating warp threads.

This is the winding of several warp threads at one time.

The warp is walked back and forth until enough threads are strung. Each time a figure eight is threaded around the rods to create a shed.

These two rods are used to string the warp (warping) so that a cross is formed between the rods forming the shed. The warp then can be transferred to lease sticks on the loom keeping alternate threads of the shed separate for stringing through heddles.

The warp is wrapped and weighted on a metal sheet (*above*) or in a box (*below*) with rocks to provide the proper tension for the warp. No wheel or rods are used to string the warp or to wrap the warp around a beam.

The new warp is tied to the ends of the old warp—first the white and then the indigo. Heddle eyes are made of nylon.

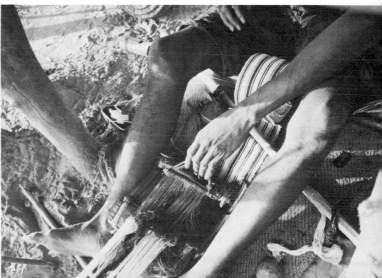

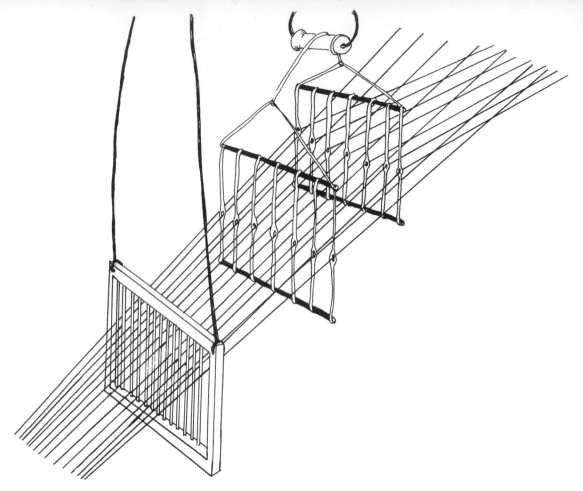

Warp is strung, diagrammed in this exaggerated view.

A weaver's view of his four-inch loom.

The weave is simple, alternating under and over, with the heddles controlled by foot rods. The reed, or batten, is controlled by the left hand, and shuttle by the right and left hand alternately.

The reed battens each weft thread to the last, creating
an even, tightly woven fabric.

Since the width is only four inches, pieces have to be sewed together. Several lengths form
enough for a woman's shawl. Here the weavers are rolling out enough for a shawl.

A length of indigo and white fabric, handwoven of handspun cotton from Tamale, Ghana.

More patterns of cotton cloth in various values of indigo and white.

A men's weave introducing a spot of red to the warp to form a stripe.

The extra heddle is used to introduce different design patterns. This design warp simply floats beneath the weaving as it is woven and is incorporated into the weave only as a shuttle bearing the weft is passed beneath them, forcing the design warp to surface to the face of the cloth. The Ashanti weavers call these "asanan" heddles. Sometimes a pick is used to pick out certain warps through which a bobbin of a different color is passed, followed by a second pick of a design weft in the alternate shed and then the regular plain weave weft.

The frame of the heddle is usually made of local twigs with multiples of strings tied with loops in the middle, the heddle eye through which warp is strung. By pedaling with sticks attached by string to the heddle or a button fitted between the toes, the shafts controlling the heddles are pulled up or down creating alternate sheds through which the shuttle-bearing weft is passed. After each pass, the reed, which is made of palm leaf ribs, is beaten against the new weft, tightening the weave. This process continues at rapid speed all day long. When the warp is finished, a new warp is attached to the old one and drawn through the heddle eyes to continue the process.

A weaver from Korhogo, Ivory Coast, using a slightly wider loom—six inches instead of four. Note the large stick of handspun cotton thread.

Six-inch widths of almost black indigo and white cotton are sewn together to form a symmetrical pattern. There does not appear to be any counting or measuring. Yet the boxes match perfectly. A testament to African weaving prowess.

TRY IT

Study the photos and create your own loom using branches and cord. You can form a pulley by stringing an empty thread spool with clothes hanger wire through a tin can. (See Ashanti improvisation.) Make certain that warp-weft (the lease in a figure 8—see diagram) is chained so that alternate warp threads can be strung through the heddle eyes without difficulty. Maintain tension by stretching the warp from a horizontal bar nearest you, the weaver, and the most distant point by use of weights. Your feet control the up-and-down movement of the heddles while your hands coordinate in rhythm by passing a shuttle wrapped with yarn through the alternating sheds. A fancy loom creates no better fabrics, if you maintain tensions and weave rhythmically, applying pressure after each pass of the shuttle, with the reed.

An Ivory Coast (Korhogo) woman's undergarment called Vwuuo. (My son absentmindedly stuck it under his belt while helping me carry other market purchases. Before long, we were surrounded by a dozen giggling women who pointed to the piece, and one man asking us where we purchased it.) The *vwuuo* top part is woven and the long strands are each braided.

An example of an ancient skill with a technological material, nylon and polyethylene monofilament woven around a thin metal bracelet blank. Accra, Ghana.

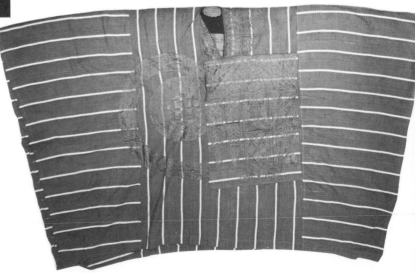

Embroidery on a Yoruba man's gown from Ibadan, southwest Nigeria.

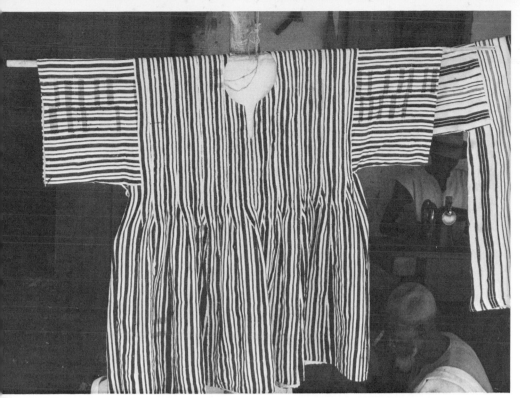

Four-inch woven indigo and cotton, sewn together to form the *damsika* for the man of northern Ghana.

The garment is then custom-embroidered by machine. Each pattern is unique.

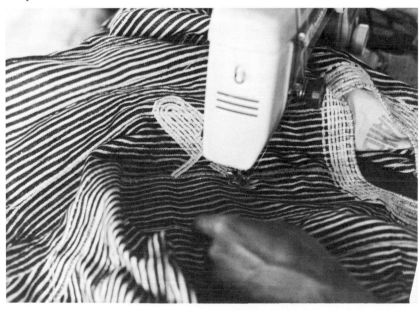

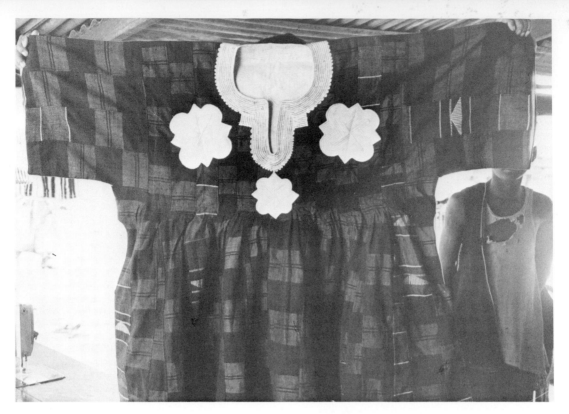

Front and back of another *damsika*.

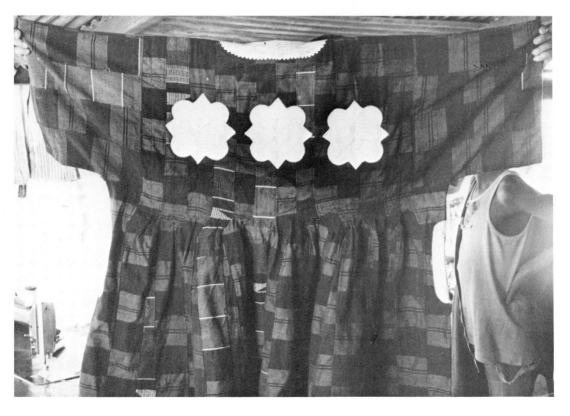

A *boubou* worn by women of the Ivory Coast. The fabric pattern is batik on a damask cotton.

A close-up showing an elegant passementerie type of machine embroidery. Whereas the style of each garment is much the same, the textile pattern and embroidery of each are very different.

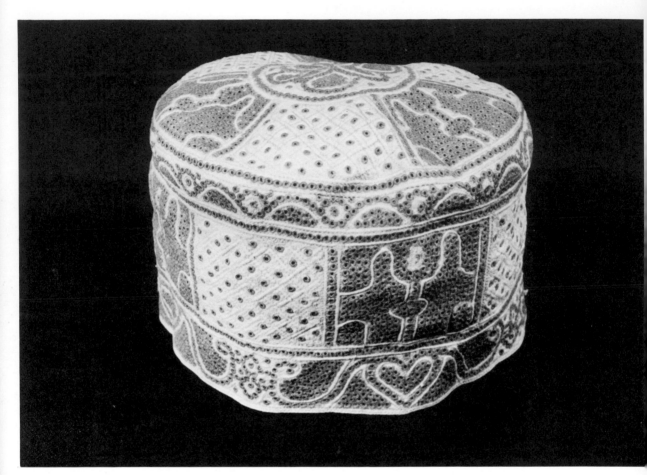

A machine custom-embroidered Moslem cap from Mombasa, Kenya.

4

/\/\/\/\/\/\/\/\/\/\/\/\

CONTAINERS: BASKETS AND CALABASHES

\/\/\/\/\/\/\/\/\/\/\/\/

Baskets and calabashes, along with ceramics, are among the earliest known man-made containers of the world. Although iron, aluminum pots, and ceramics are available for household use, the basket and calabash is ubiquitous throughout Africa. They provide countless uses for serving, storage, transporting, winnowing, and wearing. They are regarded highly and preserved. Repairs are made to calabashes in the marketplace by specialists. A calabash repairman sews together cracks with palm thread, mends other parts with bits of metal and bolts.

/\/\

BASKETRY

The materials for making baskets are everywhere, in one form or another. Grasses, willow reeds, rushes, rattan palm (cane), raffia,

Materials for making baskets are everywhere, in one form or another.

Making baskets by the Frafra of Korhogo, Ivory Coast, is a family affair.

bamboo, split palm fronds, papyrus fibers, banana fibers, swamp straw, sisal-like fibers, creepers from the forest—are some of the natural materials used by Africans to form baskets. Tools are simple, a knife and awl are all that are essential, but some people use blunt needles for sewing raffia and fibers. A calabash containing water is usually close at hand as well.

Extraordinary shapes and handsome forms are created by basket weavers. An unusual coil basketry hat, sometimes covered with leather resembling the helmets of warriors, has been used in recent years to glorify champion bush cutters. Straw and leather shapes that are meant to hang from trees or beams are used to store grain. These helmets and grain carriers are typically West African, worn and used by Tuaregs, Hausas, and people living along the old camel trade route. The women of the Abagusii tribe of the Kisii district of Kenya make baskets that have a skin base for waterproofing. The weave is so tight that these baskets are used by women for drinking millet beer. The Vambo people plait Makalani palm into baskets. The Basongye men of the Congo make raffia baskets. Each man gathers and dyes his own raffia fibers. Using four colors—natural, yellow, red, and black—he coils and embroiders very decorative shapes. (They have become a favorite of tourists.)

In Uganda, the Buganda make round and oval baskets with lids of coiled banana fibers that are bound with raffia and grass. Liberians form black-and-white twilled baskets to use as rice fanners. Baskets are used for serving coffee or nuts, millet porridge, and various other foods, storage of grains, carrying seed, grain and other harvested crops, winnowing millet and rice, fish traps, shields, quivers, boxes, costumes for ceremonies—applications that have roots in tradition and are very much a part of the life-style of Africans.

Preparation of Materials

The materials of basketry vary with the terrain and what is available locally. Basketry materials are not on import materials lists; therefore, what is used from locale to locale will differ greatly.

Natural papyrus fibers are picked when the grasses are young and are formed with water. They are sometimes lashed horizontally to a frame of vertical reeds. By dyeing the papyrus with fruit and bark dyes, ornamental stripes can be woven into the design.

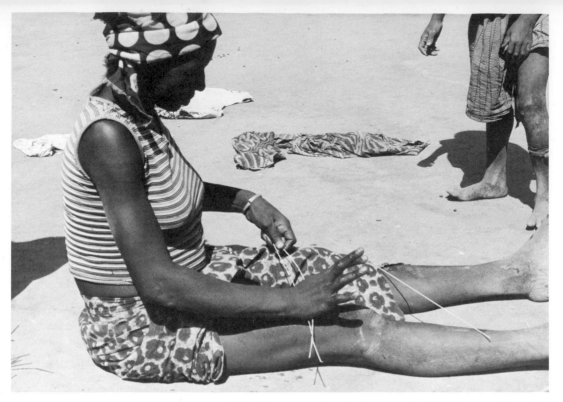

Dried river straw is rolled out on the thigh into a tight twist.

Six strands form a beginning.

The center is untwisted and six strands are slid into the opening.

Then some strands are woven one under the other.

New weavers are added as needed . . .

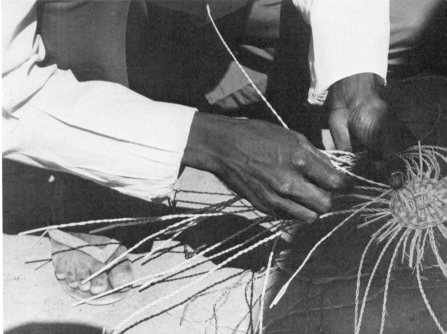

. . . and new stakes are added.

The straw is kept pliable with water. Here the piece is being immersed in water.

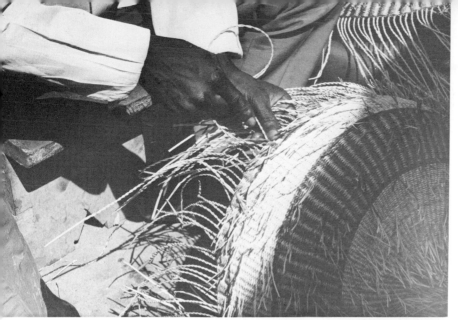

Partway up two weavers are woven alternately around stakes particularly when a different color or pattern is made.

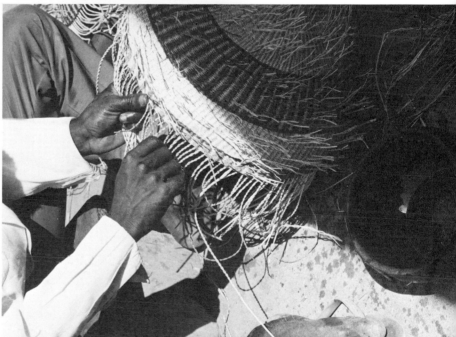

Remaining spokes are gathered and then wrapped with more river straw to form the rim.

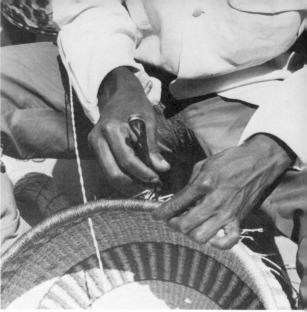

To create a handle, an awl is used to pierce a hole big enough to insert three or four pieces of straw . . .

. . . and second hole is formed for the other half.

Pieces are inserted . . .

·135

. . . gathered together around the rim and wrapped with more straw.

This continues for about two to three inches and then both sides are combined and wrapped together to form the bridge of the handle. The wrapping continues to the middle where a second half is joined and tied together.

A razor is used to cut away ends of weavers that had been left exposed.

The completed Zaara basket.

Two other designs.

The basket market in Korhogo.

Rushes (such as bulrushes—cat-o'nine-tails) are gathered before they mature and are dried slowly. They need to be used in a wet state.

Cane, which is the core of cane or the rattan palm (*Calamus rotang*), a climbing plant, extends shoots that grow to the length of six hundred feet. Leaves and thorns are peeled, and the cane is used after soaking for ten to twenty minutes in water.

Grasses of various kinds are picked before maturity and dried slowly in the shade. They are used for coils and for wrapping stiffer fibers. Generally, they need little or no water.

Bamboo is cut when shoots are green and are split. Because of brittleness, it must be kept wet when working.

Raffia is part of the frond of the raffia palm and is used in a dry state.

Willow (osiers) grown just for basketmaking comes from new shoots cut when the sap is lowest. Twigs are dried and then soaked immediately before using. If they are used immediately after cutting, no soaking is necessary. These twigs can be peeled.

Straw from wheat and other grasses is stripped of leaves and soaked in cold water for eight to twenty hours. Unthreshed straw is used for braiding because it is pliable; threshed straw is used for coarser work as a stiff material.

Palm fibers are stripped and hung to dry. They are then rolled into a cordlike material that is very hard wearing. These fibers do not have to be soaked before using.

Sisal-like fibers also are rolled into cord and used in a dry state.

Creepers from the forest are dried, split, and soaked to a pliable state before weaving.

Another style of Frafra basket. This one with stiff spokes and heavy weavers.

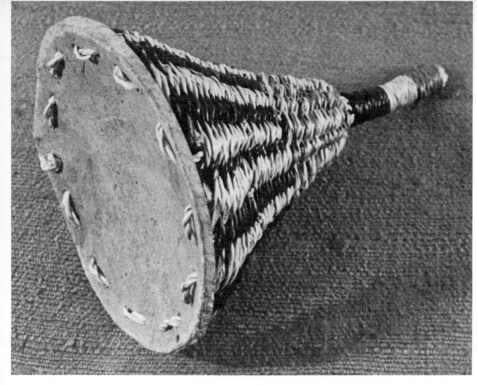

A musical instrument made with straw and sealed with the bottom of a gourd.

Basketry Construction

The most common and perhaps earliest basketry technique is the coiled basket. Basically, straw, reed, or some other base material is wrapped with raffia or grasses at the same time that coils are stitched or tied together. The base material is spiraled into a coil as it is wrapped or sewn to form a base, with successively wider coils building the forms out and progressively narrow coils reducing the circumference, creating various shapes. (See diagrams.) Very closely wrapped coils can be liquidproof, particularly if sealed with pitch. Different designs can be created by using different colors of raffia and varying the pattern as coils are wrapped.

A wickerwork type of construction uses a stiff material such as straw, cane, or reed as an inflexible, almost rigid warp (spokes or stakes), and a more flexible material as a weft (weavers) passing it over and under the spokes or stakes. Patterns are created by varying and skipping the number of stakes that the weavers pass under and over.

For forming the twined basket, which is a variation of the above, the weavers are not a single unit; two or more strands are twisted or braided around successive stakes and passed alternately over and under these spokes.

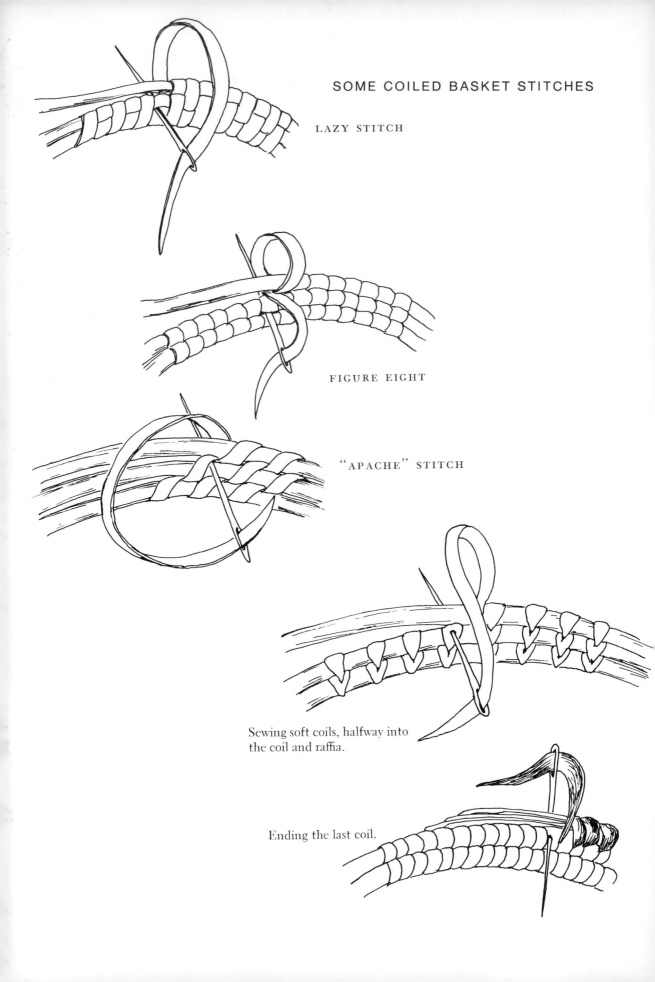

SOME COILED BASKET STITCHES

LAZY STITCH

FIGURE EIGHT

"APACHE" STITCH

Sewing soft coils, halfway into the coil and raffia.

Ending the last coil.

In wickerwork or twilled baskets, the warp and weft usually are the same material, the same size, thickness, pliability, but may be a different color. The way weft skips and hops over varying numbers of warp determines design patterns.

When starting or ending stakes and weavers, two are overlapped through two or three spokes or two or three rows of weavers. The photographed process shown here allows the new weavers to stick out (on the outside). These are cut away later. For starting a base, the number of stakes is determined by the size of the basket—more stakes for bigger shapes. There are many ways to begin. The method shown here uses an uncoiled or split center through which an equal number of stakes are passed. If stakes are thin, they can be tied or wrapped. One can start with an even number of stakes when using two weavers at the same time, or an odd number when using one. Then weaving proceeds, varying pattern or just plainly weaving under and over stakes. Finishing is by overlapping, weaving flexible ends of stakes back into themselves (the weavers) and/or by wrapping with more weaver material. One method for attaching a handle is described in these photos.

A raffia basket from Kano, Nigeria.

A wrapped raffia basket and lid from Sierra Leone. The basket is upside down in order to show the design treatment.

Straw basket from Upper Volta.

Decorative hanging Tuareg ornaments from Mali.

Coiled grass bound with raffia basket and cone-shaped lid from Kigezi, Uganda. Extremely fine baskets with geometric pattern in one darker natural color raffia. Weaving done by pastoral Watussi women, who are of Hamitic origin. Some of these baskets are fine enough to hold milk.

A very large hamper type of raffia-wrapped coiled basket from Ibadan, Nigeria. Compared to bracelets on the floor, it is at least thirty-six inches in diameter.

TRY IT

Materials that are available to most locales are twigs, vines, grasses, straw, rushes. These need to be dried, peeled, and sometimes soaked as indicated above. Some basket-weaving materials are imported and can be purchased in art and craft supply stores. Raffia is certainly available in these supply centers. Pine needles are excellent filling or base materials for wrapping with raffia into coil forms. The process is the same. No adaptations are needed. Basketry is one craft that finds counterpart techniques in both hemispheres.

A basket tray from Ruhengeri, Rwanda. *Courtesy: Smithsonian Institution*

A Somali coiled basket with decorative weaving in a light tan raffia.

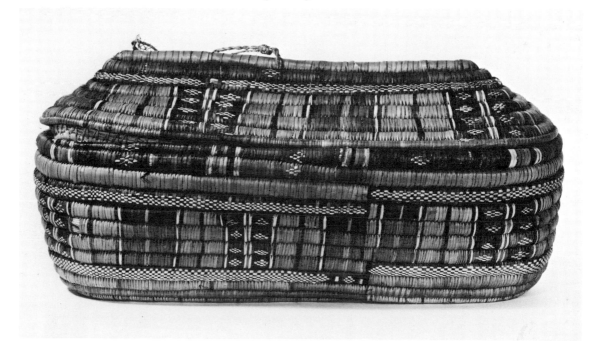

A coiled basket with lid by Zulu from Zululand, South Africa. *Courtesy: Smithsonian Institution*

Two woven elephant-hair bracelets from Kenya.
Colors are red, white, and black.

THE CALABASH

Some calabashes are undecorated and others are elaborately designed with burning, inlaying, engraving, painting, or carving. For the most part, the calabash is a container, a receptacle for something. As a storage container for water or peanut oil, or a bottle for shaking cream into butter, a dipper at the well, a basin for washing, or as a dish for eating—the calabash is a highly prized lightweight container. Sometimes, though, it is used as a decorative wall ornament, other times as a maraca-type musical instrument or a harp.

Preparing Calabashes (Gourds)

There are several ways of preparing a calabash for use and decoration. In one method (Oyo, Nigeria), fully grown calabashes are picked and soaked in water until the contents are completely rotten. Then they are opened and the insides are thoroughly cleaned out. The emptied calabashes then are left to dry in the sun.

During soaking, the skin becomes bloated and soft, but as it dries it becomes hard again so that it can be carved and worked very much like wood. The usual color is a warm yellow.

After the calabash hardens, it can be carved, engraved, burned with a hot pointed instrument, or painted.

A second method (Frafra style, Bolgatanga, Ghana), is to pick the fully grown calabash and cut the head off. When open, pour water inside. Allow seeds and contents to rot. Pour the water out and clean away the fleshy material from the inside. The gourd is allowed to dry in the sun until the shell is hard. At this point the calabash is ready to be decorated.

Calabashes cleaned, dried, and ready for carving.

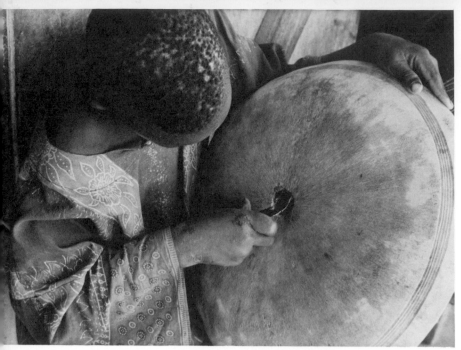

Calabash carving in Iwo, Nigeria. The only tool is a curve-bladed knife resembling the shape of a linoleum-cutting knife.

Without the aid of any drawing, circles are scribed with the tip of the knife, and then, with deeper cuts, areas are excised.

Some indications are marked on the calabash in pencil.

The design proceeds. Small triangular cuts become a diamond-shaped repeat design.

Calabash Decoration

As soon as a calabash is decorated, it is transformed from merely a useful object to a status symbol. The beautiful calabash is something one displays with pride. Designs vary from area to area and can be identified as a calabash from Oyo, a Frafra one from Bolgatanga, or a Fulbe calabash from Wangai—or wherever. Although each calabash subscribes to a local style, each can be unique as well. Seldom are patterns made beforehand to guide iron or knife. The work is sure-fingered and direct.

The Fulbe decorate gourds with hot knives. They have one knife heating in hot coals while another is being used. By drawing lines with the knives (as the Senufo do on cloth), outlines are burned into the surface. Bowls decorated in this fashion are used to bring food and delicacies to celebrations, such as weddings.

In Oyo, Nigeria, designs are carved into gourds with a knife. Outlines are made with a point of the knife, then negative shapes are carved away, leaving the positive intact. Texture, by way of lines suggesting the scales of a snake or feathers of a bird, is incised by cutting or scraping away fine lines. Sometimes the calabash is painted with enamel first and then carved, but this is a corruption of the art for the sake of attracting tourists. Some calabashes are cut all the way through to form openings, for a different effect—purely decorative.

Near Bolgatanga in the northern part of Ghana, the Frafras scratch designs into the shell of a calabash with an awl. Then they rub the design with a *shee* nut, which deposits a black brown oily substance into the engraving. In a few minutes, the excess *shee* color is rubbed off with fingers revealing darkened geometric shapes. *Wanɛ* (bowls) and *bia* (ladle) forms are popular as well as decorative. They also use violinlike snakeskin-covered gourds called *duuliga*.

Some gourds have a darker surface. This is utilized in another style of symbolic carving.

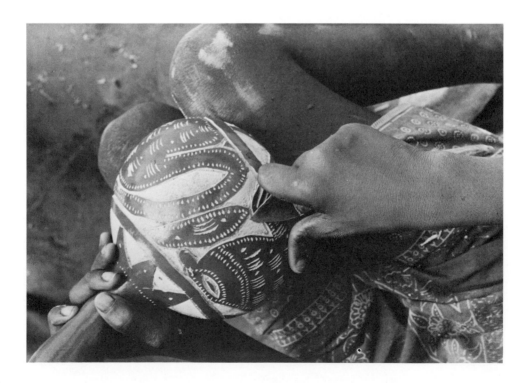

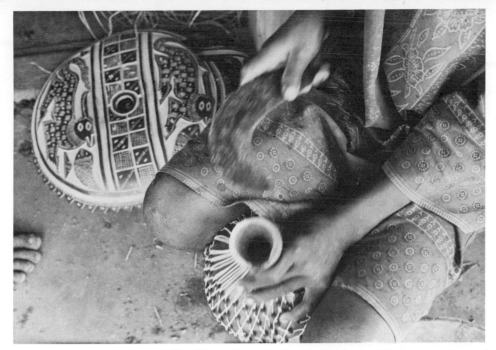

The uneven mouth of a gourd to be used as a rattle is hacked off with the same shaped knife that is larger in size.

Rattling sounds are made by seeds strung on a macramé cord design over the calabash. As the hard seeds scratch and bump against the gourd the hollow sound box created by the void in the gourd magnifies the sound.

A gigantic carved calabash from Iwo, Nigeria. It is about twenty-eight inches in diameter and about thirty-two inches high.

Another carved gourd from Nigeria.

Symbolism and geometric designs decorate this very large calabash and lid from Iwo, Nigeria. Dark lines are made with a pencil.

More carving of cala-
bash pieces. Nothing is
wasted.

The lid has a hole so that a finger can lift it off.

Small decorative carvings.

A smaller calabash and lid with openwork in the lid.

A calabash, meant as a wall hanging when not in use, is painted black before carving. Symbolism is from myths and folklore.

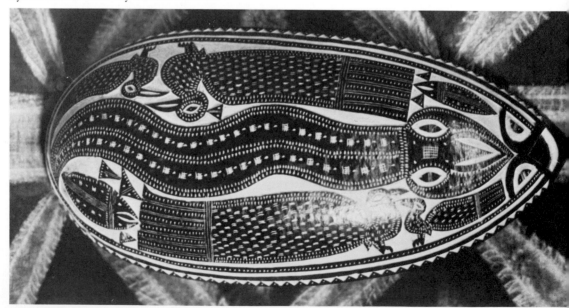

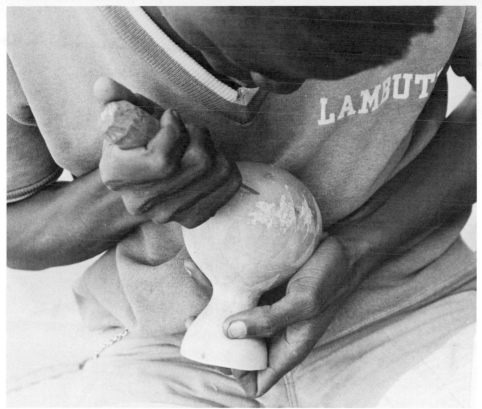

Frafra (Bolgatanga—northern Ghana) technique of calabash decoration. An awl is used to scratch or incise lines in geometric patterns or in abstract symbols on the surface.

An oily *shee* nut is used for its black brown color.

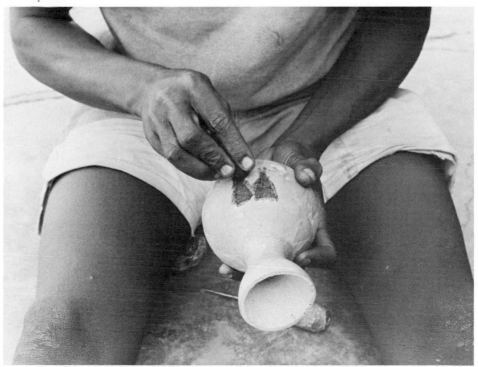

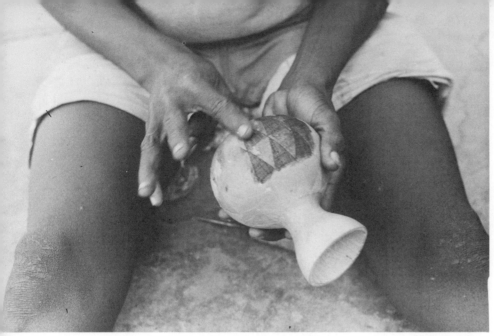

Excess is rubbed off with a finger.

Two completed calabash containers.

Two others, a bowl (upside down) and a ladle.

A kind of violin called a *duuliga*. A calabash is tautly covered with snakeskin and the rest is covered with leather. Horsetail forms the strings and the bridge is a twig.

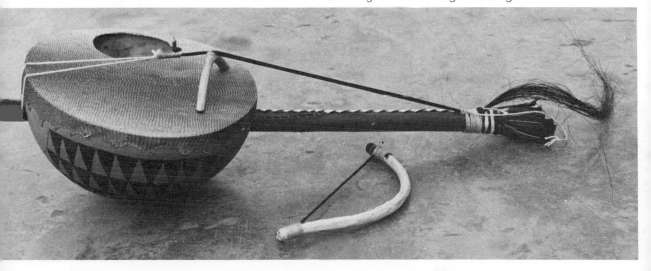

The calabash can be extended with bamboo, which is stitched on. The part that was cut off is also sewn to bamboo and it becomes the lid. These kinds of containers are highly valued all over Africa because they are strong, easy to clean, and are lightweight.

Another calabash rattle with leather trimming from Kano, Nigeria. Decorations are burned into the calabash with a hot knife.

More designs on calabashes that are incised and burned to create design.

A snuff bottle, called *ikutu*, made of a small doum palm (*Ilala*) "calabash" and fitted with a cow-horn neck. The chain and tweezers, also made by hand, are part of an old man's dress. Kamba tribe, Kenya.

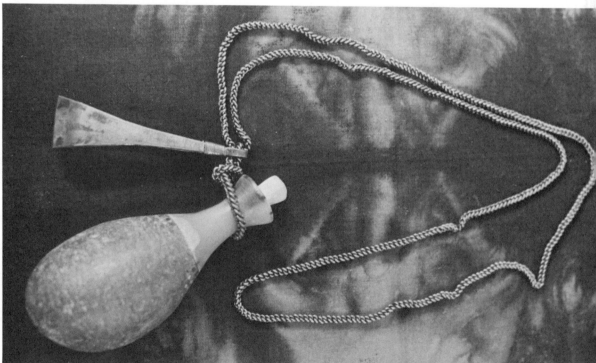

A calabash with the top wrapped in leather becoming a tight-fitting lid. Beadwork on leather and a burned-on design on the calabash complete the elegance of this traveling container for the Masai nomad's diet staple —blood and milk. It hangs over the shoulder.

Two small hollow nuts, filled with pebbles and attached with a strip of monkey fur, are a musical rattle. Pygmies of the Congo clash and rattle the nuts together.

A gourd snuff or medicine bottle decorated with silver wire. Zulu, Natal, South Africa. *Courtesy: Smithsonian Institution*

TRY IT

Calabashes of a smaller variety than those grown in Africa can be started from seed. Seed companies such as Henry Field in Shenandoah, Iowa, sell seeds (#3175 and #3172) that grow into decorative gourd shapes. These can, after preparation indicated above, be cut, carved, and incised.

This is another method for preparing calabashes or gourds. Pick your calabashes when the stems are very dry and ready to break. Take them indoors and place them over a radiator or some other heating unit, such as an oil burner, or wherever there is warmth. Every day wipe them with a cloth that has been saturated with alcohol. This takes several months if the heat is not consistent. When the seeds inside the gourd rattle as the calabash is shaken, it is ready for cutting and carving. Cut a hole in the calabash, possibly at the stem end, and shake out the seeds. Then incise and carve your designs.

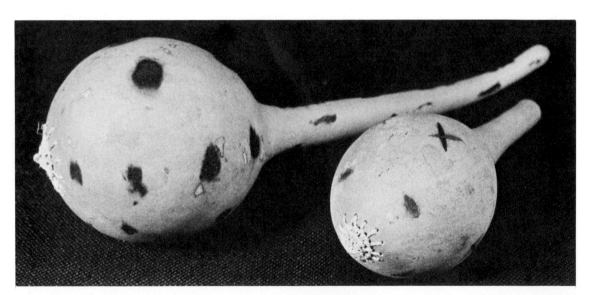

A calabash rattle about six inches long from the west Nile, Uganda. A brown gourd is cut to insert small stones and woven closed with raffia. It is decorated with a hot poker to create burned-in designs.

5

∧∧∧∧∧∧∧∧∧∧∧∧∧

HIDES, SKINS, AND FEATHERS

∨∨∨∨∨∨∨∨∨∨∨∨∨

TRADITIONS

Skins of wild animals were most probably the first clothing worn by man. Later, as animals became domesticated, man learned to utilize all animal products forming skins into clothing, foot covering, containers, tents, harnesses, and so on. Petroglyphs by Egyptians in tombs dating back to 6000 B.C. depict leather as a tribute to kings and gods. Leather sandals were important and valued in Egypt. Murals show men of rank followed by a servant carrying a pair of sandals. Princes appeared before the Pharaoh barefoot; the king alone could wear sandals —but not in the house of his gods.

Tanning of hides and skins to arrest decomposition is one of the measures of a society's place on the continuum of human development. Pieces of leather dating back to 1300 B.C. have been found in Egypt, although knowledge of tanning dates back to the Bronze Age, somewhere around 2500 B.C. Indeed, the tanning processes known to the Egyptians then are very much the same today, and are said to have spread to south of the Sahara with camel caravan trade. But these tanning skills may not have derived from the Egyptians. When the Phoenicians invaded North Africa in 1600 B.C., they brought their leather craft to the Moors. The Moors, in turn, added their ingenuity to the process and developed the famous Moroccan leather process from goatskins. (Babylonians and Assyrians used alum, oil, myrrh, and sumac to produce three varieties of leather.) Craftsmen of India also excelled in leatherworking processes. Secrets of tanning, therefore, could have come from the Moors or from India.

Tanning of leather became a secret tradition in Africa where secrets were passed down from father to son. This is still extant in Africa today. Certain families carry on these old skills as closed guilds.

⋀⋅⋁⋅⋀

USES FOR LEATHER

Fulani still make saddlebags that resemble the shikara, a traditional bag carried by men. It is elaborately adorned with leather appliqué and with leather embroidery. The Masai leather shield is tough and hard and is not unlike the early armor of the Romans and Orientals. This leather is exceedingly difficult to penetrate. Bottles were made with leather; others were covered with woven strips of leather and dried palm leaf. These are seen from Senegal to Guinea. Leather has been used, for centuries, as waterproof containers. The women of the Abagusii tribe of the Kisii district of Kenya make a millet beer pot, called ekei, that has a leather base molded and stitched over coiled basketry.

Fans of leather and parchment, some elaborately decorated, were used during ceremonies to cool the oba (king). Leather togas and aprons or skirts are worn by the Masais of Kenya, and all the way from the Sotho to the Hlubi (Zulu) of South Africa. These are often decorated with beads and cowrie shells, and sometimes with bits of metal chain. Early costumes south of the Sahara, particularly of the Hottentots, consisted, in part, of animal skins worn over one shoulder. The more wealthy folk wore wild animal pelts, and the poorer people used sheepskin. Women wore many hard-leather bracelets around their ankles. These bracelets had two uses: they were jangled during dancing and at other times served to keep their lower legs from getting cut from thorns and brush. The more rings a woman wore, the higher her status. *Samara* are tough sandals made from uncured leather.

Leather is used to encase charms called griggris, or saphies. These are bits of paper covered with sentences from the Koran that are folded and encased in leather. Africans believe in their potency as a protector from all sorts of harm and to bring the wearer good luck, many wives, wealth, and so on. Where there is Islamic influence, prayer rugs may be made from sheepskin or less frequently from calfskin and antelope hide.

The Mandingos dye leather into bright colors and carefully tan leather until it is soft and pliable. Sandals, quivers, sheaths for knives, belts, pockets, fetishes, or saphies (griggris) are some of their craft forms. The Tuaregs, Fulbes, and Hausas make an enormous variety of things of leather—tents, sacks, sandals, hats, containers for tea and sugar, tubes of sheep or goatskin for *gerbas*—containers for carrying water. Although there are indigenous design styles that are similar among these groups, there also are fine differences in interpretation that distinguish the work of the Hausa, Fulbe, and Tuareg.

In Agades, the Marabouts make boxes of parchment over clay. Leather pillows, hassocks, and camel saddles are amply used by nomads in their tents and their clothes are stored in leather bags.

This Masai leather shield is tough and hard, not unlike the early armor of the Romans and Orientals.

Fulani still make saddlebags that resemble the *shikara*. Narrow strips of leather are used to embroider this bag. Fringing, flapping with every movement, helps keep insects away.

Bottles, such as this one from Senegal, are covered with leather. Sections of leather have been slit and dried palm fibers woven in and out creating a pattern.

A basket beer pot called an *Ekei*, made by the women of the Abagusii tribe of the Kisii district in Kenya, Africa. These baskets have a skin base with hair left intact; they are used by women for drinking millet beer.

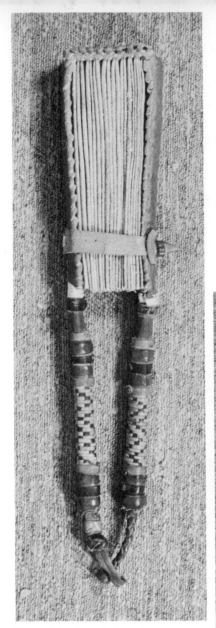

Fans of leather and parchment were used during ceremonies to cool the oba. Every part of this fan is made of leather. The accordion-pleated section is parchment.

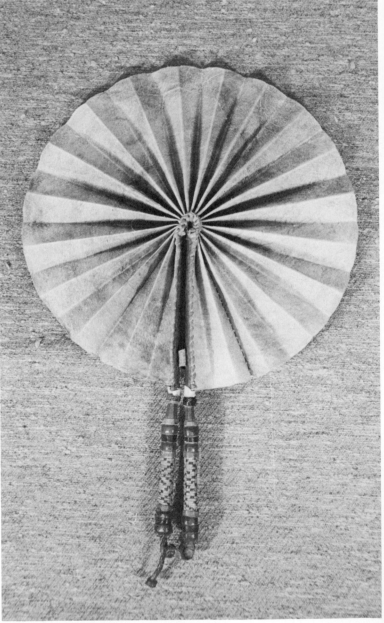

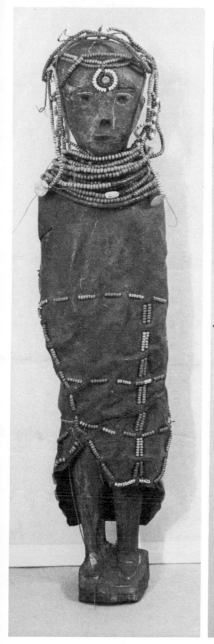
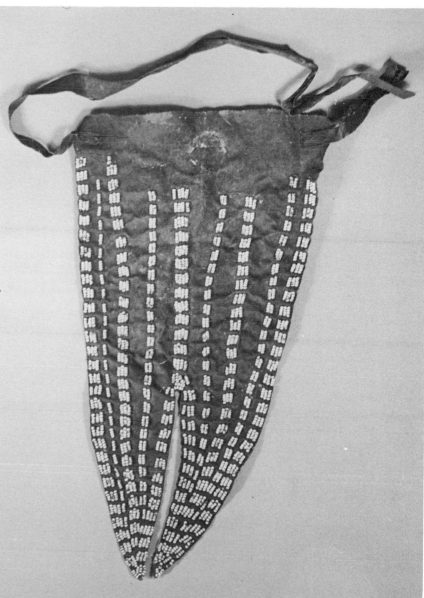

Leather togas and aprons or skirts are worn by the Masai of Kenya and the Sotho all the way down to the Zulu of South Africa. They are often decorated with beads and sometimes with bits of metal chain. The Masai lady's skirt is from the Rift Valley Province in Kenya. And the wooden doll wearing a leather toga is a Turkana doll from Anand.

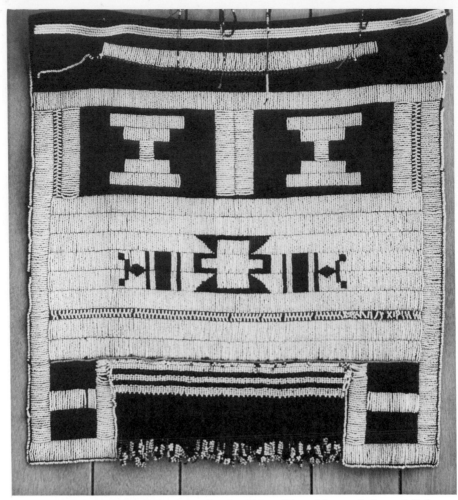

This lady's apron is Ndebele, from South Africa. Bits of brass chain and links are sewn along with beads as edging.

A woman's dress called *vwuuo* in leather. It is usually worn at a "death" ceremony. Bolgatanga, Ghana.

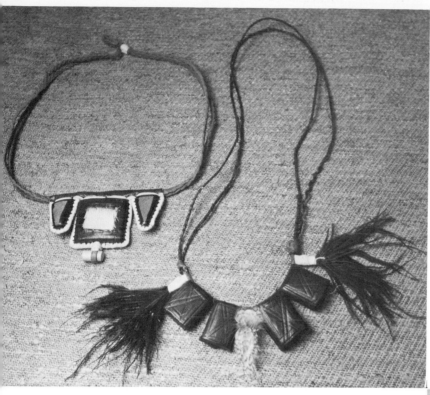

Grigris, or *saphies*, contain sayings from the Koran that are encased in leather. Africans believe in their potency as a protector from all sorts of harm, to bring the wearer good luck, many wives, wealth, and so on.

A particularly handsome Tuareg storage container for sugar from Timbuktu, Mali. The interior, or base, is wrapped raffia. The bag is constructed so that it can hang on a tree limb or beam, away from marauding insects and animals. Decoration is by direct dyeing of color.

A leather money purse in traditional design but with white plastic weaving. From northern Ivory Coast or Mali.

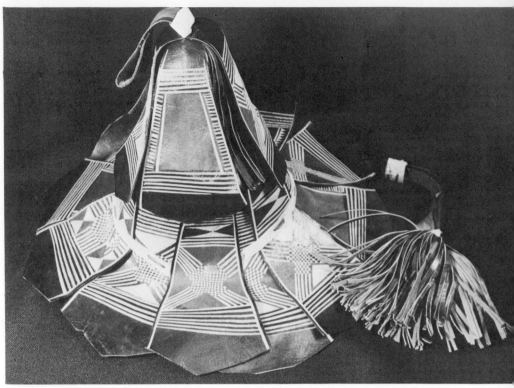

A man's hat in leather formed over woven straw. Various styles of this hat are worn by the Hausa, Fulani, and Tuareg. Decorations are made by slicing and then peeling away the very top skin layer of leather.

Leather fan from Benin, Nigeria. Fans are carried by nobles and chiefs to keep the oba cool during ceremonies. Embroidery is mainly a crewel stitch with thin leather lacing. The outside stitching is a simple overcast stitch. Hair is left intact on the background leather.

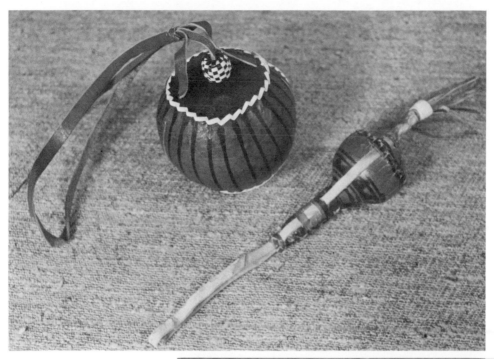

A closed and open version of perfume and cosmetic containers made of leather-covered parchment. Parchment is soaked in water, cleaned, and molded over clay. Leather is covered over the parchment base much the same way.

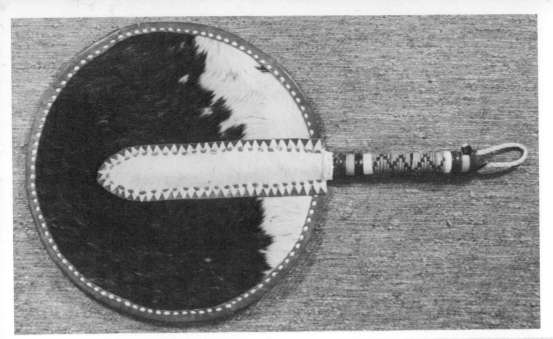

Another fan, with hair intact, from northern Nigeria. The handle is woven leather.

Suk men from Anand who have many heads of cattle are privileged to wear this Suk wig around their arm. It is made of ostrich feathers attached to leather.

Rather rare now because it is made of ostrich plumes, which are "environmentally protected," this is a Masai headpiece from Ngethe. It is held together with leather and trimmed with beads.

/.\./\\.\
PROCESSES

Whether rawhide, parchment, or dressed leather, animal skins with or without hair intact are very popular materials. Goat, sheep, camel, and bovine are the most popular kinds of leathers, although hippopotamus, buffalo, antelope, zebra, and elephant are also used—sometimes illegally. Leather from small animals is called *skins*, and from large animals, *hides*.

The preparation of skins and hides requires the scraping away of the fatty layer under the skin, cutting away the hair (some tribes use urine to speed up the process of hair removal). Then the skin is washed and dressed, sometimes by rubbing in various oils such as egg yolks, tallow, or brains and the liver of cattle. Some groups use a salt and alum dressing—but this is *tawing* and not *tanning*. Since tawing is a reversible process, the treatment wears away in time. Tanned skins are infused with sumac and oak for long periods of time. Tannin forms a chemical bond and preserves the skin. When mimosa, babul, or clutch, mangrove, or the bark of larch is used, leathers tend to become a dark red. After infusion, leathers are sometimes treated with oil dressings.

Although there are more modern tanning processes (such as chrome tanning) today, vegetable tanning is still the essential process in Africa. The procedure takes a long time, but sometimes there are shortcuts taken, particularly by nomadic groups. Preparing rawhide is faster. Rawhide is untanned cattlehide that is dehaired and limed with little else done to it. It is quite stiff. Parchment also is stiff, made from the split skins of sheep, exposed for a long time to lime, scraped and rubbed smooth. Neither of these two forms is leather, in the strictest sense of the word, because they are not preserved by dressing into a stable, nonputrescible, *flexible* sheet.

Working with Leather

As with all other African craft forms, tools are minimal and simple. Muscle power predominates over machine power. An awl, knife, and smooth polishing stone may be the only implements.

After the hide has been tanned and dyed, it is bought by craftsmen who usually work in small groups. The leather is dampened with damp sand by spreading the sand over the leather and allowing it to sit that way for about an hour. Then it is worked to a smooth finish by rubbing it with a smooth stone. This also makes the leather more pliable.

Parts of the object are cut to size by using a craft paper or cardboard pattern and slicing around it with a sharp knife. Patterns are then sketched onto the top (skin) surface of the leather with a knife, if it is to be incised; or smaller shapes are appliquéd onto the base piece using thin leather strips (thonging) in an overcast stitch. Someone might be cutting thin strips of leather from a bigger piece (thonging) for this purpose.

After individual parts have been decorated, seams that need to be joined by gluing are adhered with a gummy millet paste (but a kind of rubber cement is used near big cities where it is more readily available). Holes are made with an awl for stitches, and lacing or thonging is used to join parts, threaded through the holes. Sometimes a hand-running stitch is used on the flesh (under) side, using a heavy thread. Seams are pounded into shape and thinness with a stick, stone, hammer, or mallet. If many parts have to be joined at one seam, edges may be thinned by skiving away thin slivers of excess flesh on the flesh side, so that the leather is thinner in the area of the seam. When all the parts are joined, the object is ready, unless attachments such as closings are needed.

Whereas most leather objects are made by cutting, sewing, and pounding, rawhide, a leather that has not been oil-dressed, is shaped by soaking it in very hot water, followed by pressing it into or over a shape and tying it into that position until it dries into the molded shape.

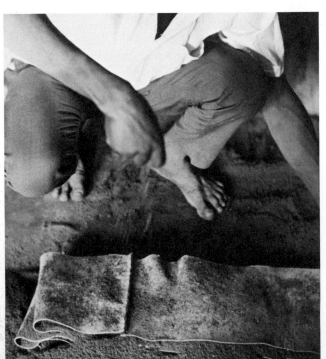

Working with leather is much the same in Mali, Upper Volta, northern Ivory Coast, Ghana, and Nigeria. In this photo, a craftsman is sprinkling dampened sand over a piece of leather.

After dampening, the leather is placed on a wooden board and then burnished with a stone. This makes the leather more pliable, works out wrinkles and makes the skin easier to peel from the flesh part of the leather for decoration.

Thonging is made by slicing thin strips of leather. Note that an awl is used to anchor the leather onto a board, while a knife is being drawn away from it.

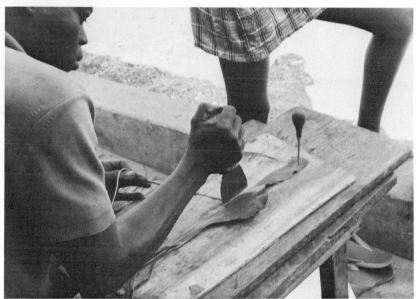

In order to create the contrasting design on the dark red leather, shallow cuts are sliced into the leather skin, usually in parallel directions.

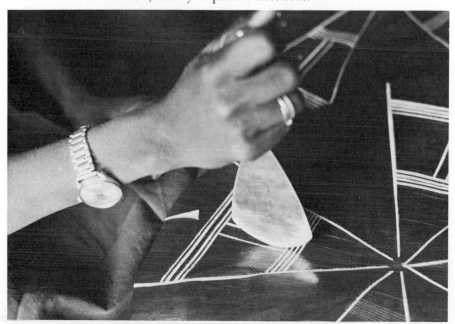

Then with the tip of a pointed knife, or with an awl, the surface skin is peeled off, revealing the whitish flesh of the leather.

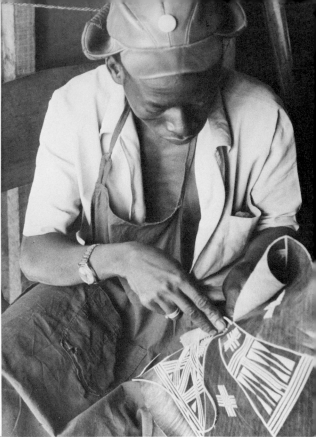

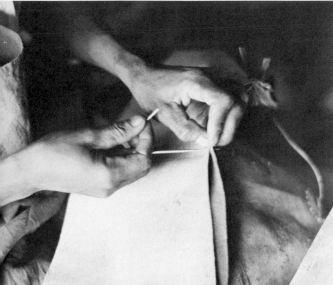

After decorations have been made on all parts, pieces are then matched, and stitch by stitch sewn together. The first step in sewing is to pierce the two parts with an awl to form a hole large enough for the waxy cotton thread.

Then the thread is strung through the hole in either an overcast, or a running stitch, as in this case.

When all parts have been attached, the assembled hassock looks like this—after it has been stuffed, of course!

Embroidery on leather is very characteristic of leather work from just south of the Sahara, north to the Mediterranean Sea. The process is simple, either with a single color, or by adding different colors of leather as in appliqué, outlines of designs are embroidered using very narrow leather strips. A hole is pierced into the leather so that the narrow leather thonging can be strung through the hole left by the awl.

Here the craftsman is pulling the leather thonging through the hole . . .

. . . and back under. Stitches are made in and out—in an overcast stitch.
Ends of thonging are tucked under other stitches and new pieces are begun
the same way.

Designs are essentially geometric with embroidered stitches of leather sewing
to accent and outline parts of the design.

Ornaments and outside attachments are made by cutting the leather to shape and size . . .

. . . applying glue, which is often a millet paste.

A hammer pounded along seams and over the piece flattens the leather and helps to adhere parts.

With a bit more trimming using a knifc, and perhaps the addition of a braid or tassel of leather, the piece is ready for attachment.

Another completed hassock, sporting embroidery and trimmings. Aside from a different decorative design and process, assembling this hassock was the same as the other one.

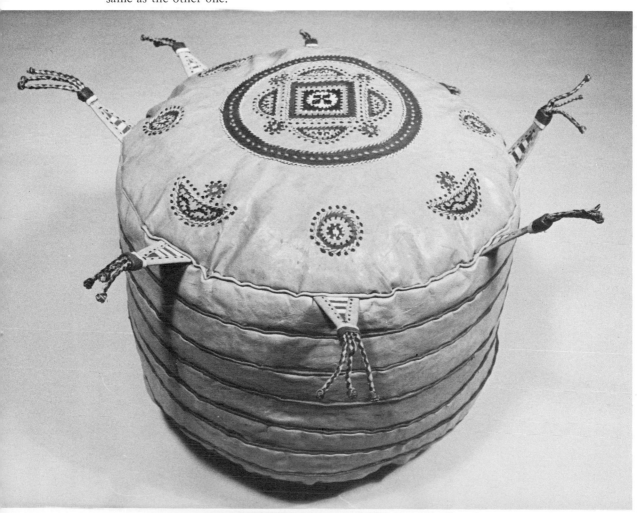

Decorating Leather

Several techniques are used—painting with knives, brushes, and dye; batik, which is using wax to temporarily preserve the base color, dyeing the rest a different color and then removing the wax; appliqué, which involves superimposing pieces of leather over one another, and reverse appliqué, which is cutting away shapes and putting a different color behind it; incising, which usually involves outlining areas with a knife and then peeling away the top surface to reveal an undyed layer beneath; and embroidery with thin, different color, narrow strips of leather. Patterns are also achieved by weaving leather strips under and over parallel slits in the leather. Fringes of leather are also very popular as edging.

The use of beads, feathers, and skins combined with and without hair; also wrapping handles in a weaving technique, are other ways of decorating leather. More details are described in the picture captions. Colors used are usually red, black, cream (natural), and Kano green.

Leather that is used to hold liquids is usually lined with pitch for waterproofing.

This is either a Maure or a Fulbe pillow using transparent lacquerlike colors in reds, greens, and yellows, outlined with black, knife-drawn lines.

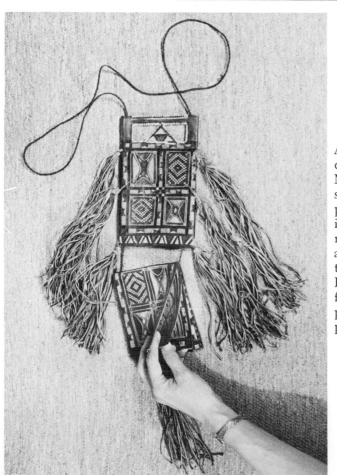

A magnificent Tuareg shoulder-strap man's purse from Mali showing the outside sleeve and a "multitude" of pockets, with flaps, on the inside wallet. Designs are made by slicing and peeling and then painting some of the flesh parts with color. Patterns are different on each flap, acting as an identifying pattern for each of the three pockets.

TRY IT

Instead of millet paste for gluing, use a rubber cement or, even better, the kind used by your shoemaker. One brand name is Barge cement. Sewing is accomplished the same way, but you can use a sewing machine. Dacron-covered threads are very good; so are wax-coated heavy button threads. Hammering of seams can be done with hammer or mallet over a hard wooden surface. Cut with a sharp knife by placing the leather over a sheet of heavy cardboard or Neolite, so as not to dull the knife. Aniline dyes, solvent type marking pens, and batik dyes are some of the colorants one can use. Treat the final piece with some paste wax to help preserve your finish.

A nontraditional belt made by Fulbe using traditional designs and embroidery with leather.

Another contemporary adaptation of African leatherwork, not from North Africa, as one would suspect, but from northern Nigeria.

A stuffed leather bracelet from Mali.

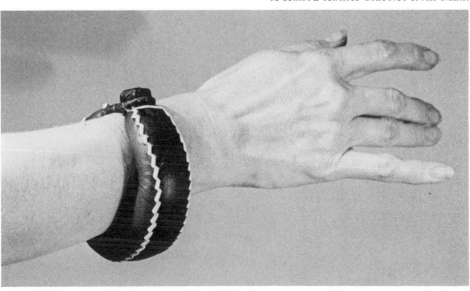

A more traditional Fulbe purse using appliqué and embroidery.

A tray in leather with leather strips woven in and out through narrow parallel cuts in the leather. From Timbuktu, Mali. The background is saffron yellow, the weaving black and red.

Three leather bracelets from Tamale, Ghana, decorated with painted designs. The button closings are made of leather as well.

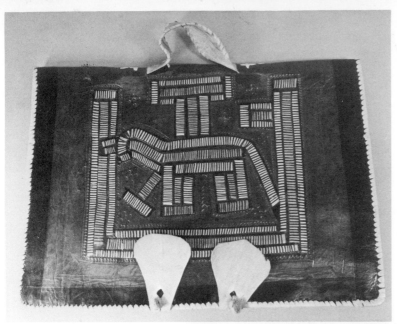

Three aspects of a leather briefcase from Mali showing the same woven decoration as in the tray. Florentine edging is used around the outside edge, covering with its wide flat overcast stitch all raw edges. No metal parts are used, only leather. Note the closing flaps.

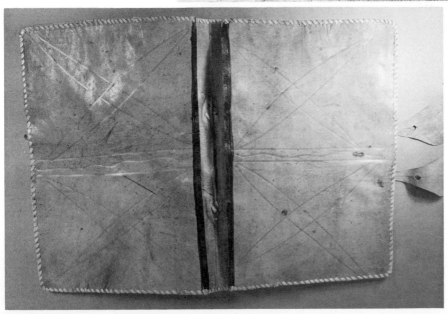

6

ΛΛΛΛΛΛΛΛΛΛΛΛ

BEADS,
SHELLS,
AND BONES

WWWWWWWWWW

THE UBIQUITOUS BEAD

Beads have been fought for, loved for, begged for, traded for, and prayed for. To some people, beads have strange powers as amulets and also provide a means of solving problems of great social dimension. Beads are like the bread crumbs tossed by Hansel and Gretel; they indicate the path of early trade routes.

By the end of the second millennium B.C., glass beads became common in the Near East, but had already been manufactured in Egypt in the Fifth Dynasty. Egyptian blue faience was very highly valued. Camel routes and sea routes transmitted beads from Egypt, Venice, India, Portugal, and Holland throughout Africa. Origins of these beads can usually be traced, but the source of one bead remains a mystery—it is the aggri. West Africans think of the aggri bead as magical and capable of miracles because very old beads have been

Cowrie shells were used not only for ornament, decoration, and ritual, but had extrinsic value as well, as a medium of exchange. This cowrie shell necklace and back ornament is combined with leopard teeth, another symbol of power. From the Congo.

dug from the ground. Africans believe aggri beads generate from the soil. These beads vary in color and sometimes have variegated designs made of a glass or porcelain-like material. Most experts believe the aggri bead to be of Egyptian origin. A single aggri bead was so valued by an Ashanti, it was reputed to have been exchanged for seven brides. One bead given a bride on her wedding day is a highly valued present.

Beads were an important item in the slave trade exchange, and kings who fattened their coffers on this kind of trade lived opulently, bedecked with beads. (Beads covered bodies, thrones, stools—everything.) Cowrie shells also made up part of this exchange. They were used not only for ornaments, decoration, and ritual use, but were a medium of exchange. Strung together, they were used as money. Cowries could buy slaves and also brides. They are still seen inland in the market areas, used as small change.

The cowrie shell had religious significance because of its shape, which has a feminine image. They often form part of sacrificial offerings and are used for mask ornamentation and for ceremonial wear on costumes. Senufo men and girls wear belts of cowries during their period of initiation rites. And the Bete of the Ivory Coast wear belts of cowrie shells for war dances.

Beads help distinguish one group from the other in the same way as does the cicatrization, or welting on faces and bodies, to beautify and identify. Beads are coordinated with these patterns and complete the appearance of beauty and tribal identification. Bushmen of South Africa still undergo welting on their faces and bodies. They consider bare skin ugly and want to be as beautiful as the animals that have patterned skins such as zebras. They wear quantities of beads made from ostrich eggshells, approximating their ideal of beauty, the zebra. Not only did beads and bead patterns create distinctions between tribes, but they also denoted differences among castes within a tribe. At the top, certain beads and patterns were reserved for royalty.

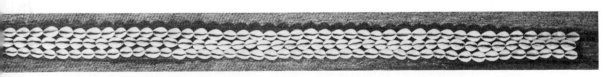

Senufo men and girls wear belts of cowries during their period of initiation. And the Bete of Ivory Coast sport belts of cowrie shells for war dances.

As decoration, cowries are attached to this raffia basket from Nigeria.

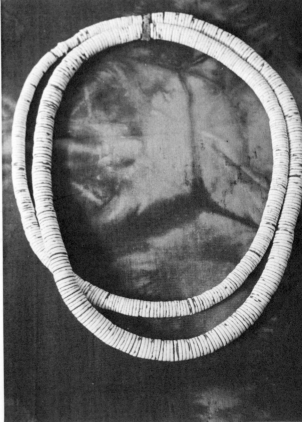

Bushmen of South Africa wear quantities of beads made from ostrich shells as do Turkana ladies and young mothers of northern Kenya. Disks are cut from ostrich eggshells.

⋀⋀⋀
KINDS OF BEADS

Cowries, ostrich shell and glass beads, are not the only kinds of beads. There are beads made not only of other kinds of shells, but of bone, animal teeth such as leopards, which are considered potent, and beads of reed and straw, bronze, gold (rarely), silver, ivory, stone, seeds, and tusks. There are semiprecious materials too. The Fulani wear quantities of heavy amber beads. Carnelian beads are found in East Africa along the coast and along the fringes of the camel route in northern Ivory Coast, Ghana, and Nigeria. Warriors of the Neyo, Bete, Godie, Bakive, Kru, and others believe that a scarlet shell found by river people of the Sassandra region of the Ivory Coast is imbued with supernatural qualities. They use bits of these shells on their weapons. Jasper, coral, and carnelian have been worn by the kings of Nigeria as emblems of their authority. Until two centuries ago, crowns of the obas (divine kings) of Nigeria were made of red carnelian, agate, jasper, and Balearic coral—all were of local origin, except the coral. Small beads came later as a peacocklike adornment of kings. Polishing of beads often was under the king's patronage.

A lightweight, delicate necklace of reed from Kenya, probably Turkana or Suk.

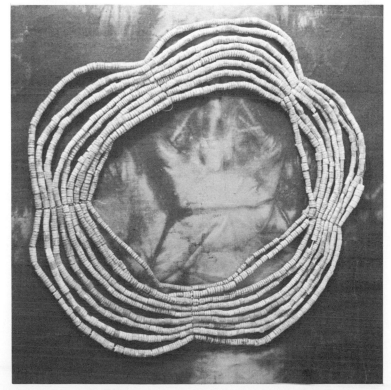

Beads made of bone and animal teeth, such as leopard, are considered potent.
That makes this necklace of the Luba powerful "medicine."

Golden glossy straw wrapped and pressed into shaped beeswax provides a handsome substitute for the gold that it imitates. Dogon and Tuareg of Mali.

The Fulani wear quantities of amber beads. These were from the Ivory Coast. Each bead is about one to one and one-half inches in diameter.

The Yoruba of Nigeria, Dahomey, Togo, and Ghana (Ife was their heritage) have a rich mythology that can be splendidly portrayed with the pattern and colors of beads. To this day, their art and craft display a kind of symbolic and surrealistic vitality that is as alive and fresh as it was in the days when Ife was at its prime. New and original ideas are emerging constantly.

The Yoruba of Nigeria, Dahomey, Togo, and Ghana have a rich mythology that can be splendidly described and implemented with the patterns and colors of beads. This ostrich and bead fan is from Nigeria.

A linguist's staff from Nigeria. Carved wood is wrapped with cloth and each bead is spot-stitched or lazy-stitched to the cloth. The donkey symbol is attached to the staff with metal bars.

A fly whisk adorned with a beaded handle. From Nigeria.

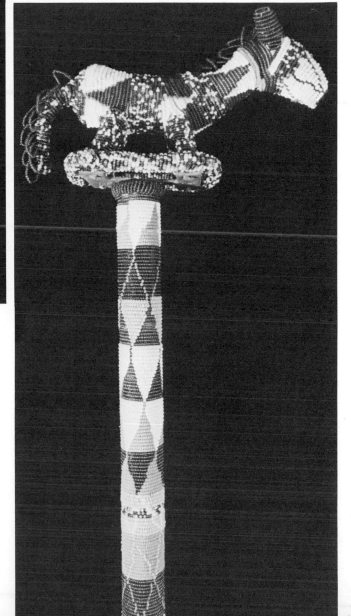

The people of Cameroon also use bead trimming. Like the Yoruba, it was at first reserved for the court. The Bamum decorate calabashes with beads and also make dolls that are covered with beads and cowrie shells.

The people of Cameroon also use beads much like the Yoruba. Beads in Cameroon were at first reserved for the court. But later people like the Bamum decorated calabashes and dolls, as shown here, with beads and cowrie shells or seeds. The base is wood, covered with cloth, to which beads and seeds are sewn.

The Masai of East Africa create splendid beaded collars with beads strung between and on wire rings. At least three or four of these are worn at once. And, for festive occasions, the size goes beyond twenty-four inches in diameter. The ubiquitous calabashes the nomadic Masai use to carry their blood-milk food drink, while they are on the road, are also decorated with leather and beads. So are their togas. The Zulu of South Africa are among the greatest artists with beads. Aprons, clothing, coverings, and house ornaments predominate.

Most tribes use beads, shells, and bones as ornamentation and costume. As jewelry, it is utilized to encircle some part of the body—neck, waist, ankles, legs, arms, fingers. They decorate and protect with their spiritual charms—and are considered to be extremely erotic.

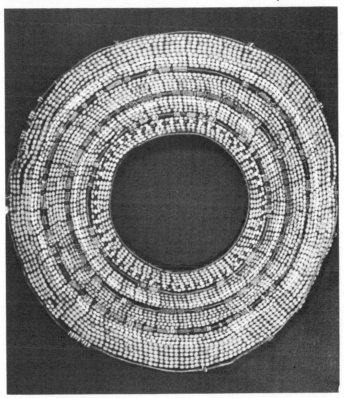

The Masai of Kenya create splendid beaded collars, strung on wires and supported by heavy wire rings so that they stand out from around the neck rather than drape around the neck and shoulders. This is a huge dancing necklace that weighs about eight pounds.

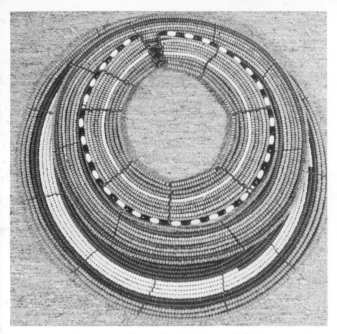

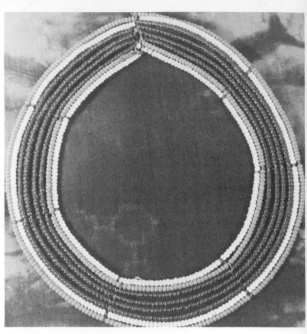

A group of smaller Masai necklaces worn in a cluster that form a collar. Different smaller necklaces are combined for everyday wear.

A small, single unit Masai necklace-collar.

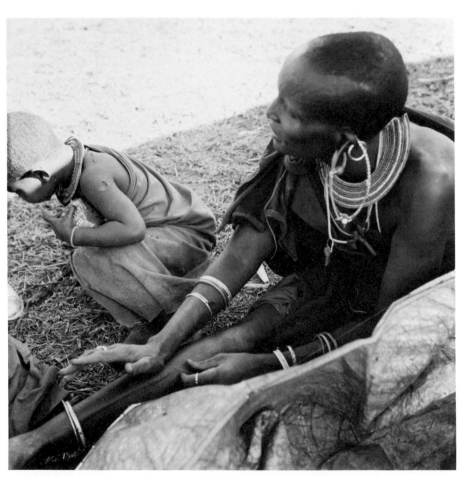

A Masai woman from near Ngorongoro, Tanzania, rolling palm fiber on her leg to join one end to another.

The fiber is then threaded through a needle . . .

. . . and each bead is sewn on separately. The ladies are sewing beads on rawhide, in the shade of their loaf-shaped homes.

Stripes of beads and outlines of edges complete the toga design. The child standing near the mother sports a cotton toga.

Besides decorating leather in various ways and making collars, the Masai also string beads on thread, wear that around their necks and decorate children with them as well.

Some of the beads may also find their way into tourist markets.

The Zulu of South Africa (this is Ndebele village) are among the greatest artists with beads. Aprons, ornaments, fly whisks, and belts match the geometric patterns on their houses.

A Ndebele apron of beads and bits of metal chain on leather. The lazy stitch was used to attach the beads to the background.

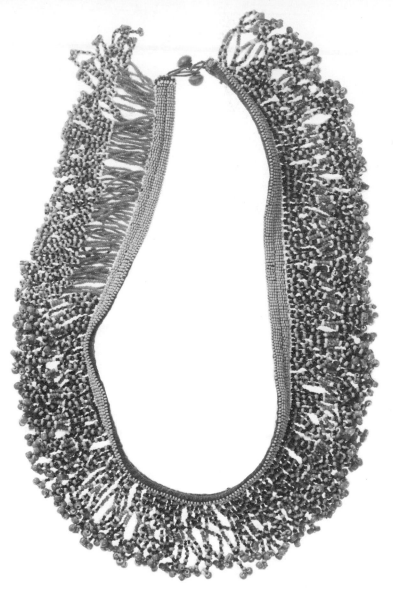

Bead girdle, Zulu, South Africa. *Courtesy: Smithsonian Institution*

A Chiwamba dance form worn by the Matushi dancers under their buttocks. Luvali tribe.

PATTERNS OF BEADS

Beads of various materials have their own intrinsic qualities. The famous African trade beads that come from Europe, mainly Holland, come in various patterns and colors. Among these are the Venetian bugles, inlaid and fused with millefiori patterns called "eyes," which were in great demand even before the 1700s. Glass beads, homemade in Bida, Nigeria, from scrap glass of various colors, were also popular for their color and patterns. (Their entire output today is mostly for the tourist trade.) Ivory beads along with the teeth of wild boars, human bone, horn, and ostrich eggshell, shapes of bronze formed by the lost-wax process, feathers, and reed make for a rich and varied supply.

Beads are tiny, flat, fat, round, square, hexagonal, irregular, opaque, transparent, hard, dull or bright in color, increasing the creative possibility and the potential for uniqueness. Most popular, though, are tiny imported glass beads that come in many colors. They can be woven, sewed, strung, and tied in an endless variety of patterns, mostly geometric.

Hand-carved ivory beads are strung on palm fiber in this Bwamé bracelet from Lega.

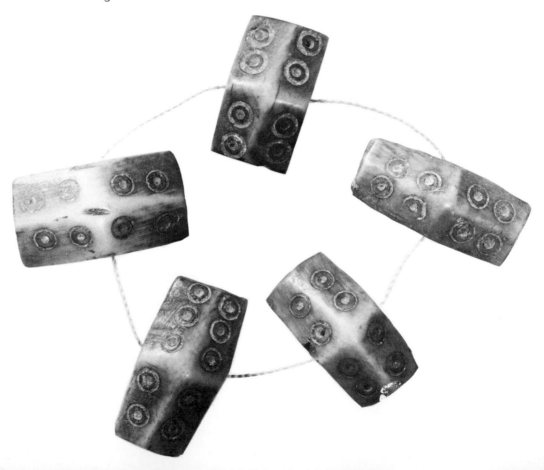

On the left is a Masai head-dress from Mburu, Kenya. And on the right are the African trade beads that are ubiquitous in West Africa. These trade beads are imported from Europe. The eye and beads composing much of the necklace are made of fused Venetian millefiori pieces of glass bugles.

A bamboo-and-horn Swazi necklace from South Africa.

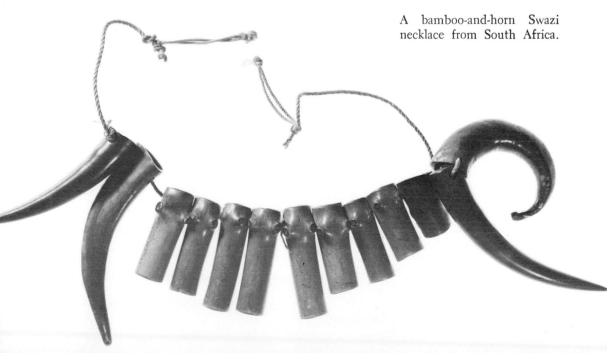

.λ.λ.λ.
PROCESSES

Beads are usually strung on the tough fiber made from rolling dried palm leaves on the thigh, or the fiber of other vegetable or plant products. More recently cotton and nylon have been employed. Wax is used to stiffen the tip for stringing; but needles are necessary when beads are attached to cloth, leather, or raffia.

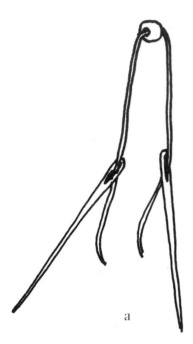

a

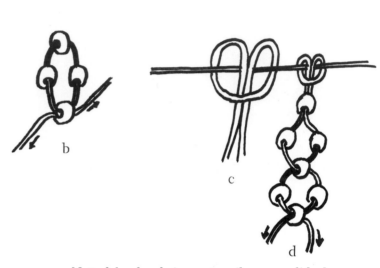

b

c

d

Netted beadwork is most easily accomplished using two needles (a). Diagram b describes the direction of bead stringing. Figure c illustrates how strands can be attached to a neckline strand using a macramé knot. And d shows how to utilize the two strands that have been knotted.

Diagram e is lazy stitching describing how strands are attached to a background.

Diagram f is bead weaving, with beads woven in and out between strands of warp. A second run-through with the needle (as shown here) anchors and reinforces the weaving.

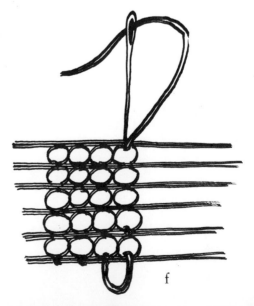

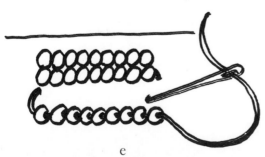

e

f

Woven Beadwork

Beads can be woven in and out of warp using thread. A board is all that is necessary to form a loom. Warp strands are stretched end to end. The weft is made of beads that are woven in and out of the warp. Sometimes thread is passed through the bead holes a second time to strengthen the weft.

A Pokomo necklace (Tana River, Kenya), called *kishinda*, made by women using beads threaded on thin fiber or sisal thread. The piece is woven ending with a fringe of beads and small shells. These necklaces are worn by married women for special dances and on ceremonial occasions.

Another style of woven glass bead necklace made by the Pokomo. *Courtesy: Smithsonian Institution*

A Tembu bead collar, formed by weaving beads. From the Transkei, East Pondoland, South Africa. *Courtesy: Smithsonian Institution*

Spot Stitching

In spot stitching, two threads can be used. The beads are strung on a thread in the desired color and pattern order. Then after every two or three beads a second thread is used to fasten the first string to the backing. Linear, curved, circular, and filled designs are possible this way. Before a needle and thread, wax or pitch was used to stiffen the thread, and a pointed instrument like a bone fragment was used like an awl to pierce a hole.

Spot stitching is also possible by stitching each bead on the backing, one at a time.

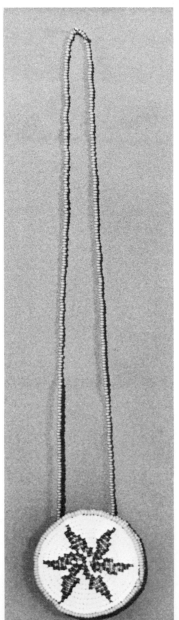

Almost universal, a contemporary bead ornament made by spot stitching beads onto a cloth disk; made in Nigeria.

Netted Beadwork

Netted beadwork is created in a variety of ways to produce either a lacy netlike pattern or closely woven design, depending on how threads are restrung through the beads to reverse directions and create patterns and whether one or two needles are used. Cape collars and coverings for round objects are made this way because a bias is formed that drapes easily around curved forms.

A netted beadwork necklace can be started using two needles, one on each end on a single length of thread. Patterns are created by having both needles go through the same beads, then branch out and come together again. The threads are begun by usually looping it around a braided and strung base that fits around the neck. Sometimes strands are attached to the neckline base using a macramé knot.

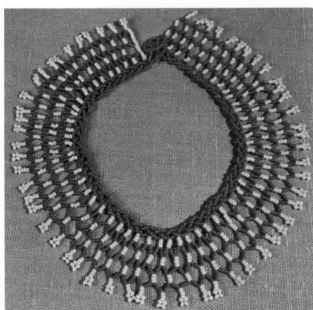

A Zulu netted beadwork necklace.

Zulu netted beadwork house ornaments.

Lazy Stitching

Lazy stitching is the fastening of beads in short, close, parallel rows only at the ends. The needle and thread are positioned and sewn through the fabric or leather. Then the desired amount of beads are strung; at this point, the needle is pushed through the fabric, fastening the row of beads and accommodating the number of beads that have been strung. In this case, beads are anchored only at the ends of the rows. Geometric designs result in this method.

Beads lazy stitched on leather from Korhogo, Ivory Coast.

Shells and Bones

Holes are usually drilled through shells and bones so that they could be strung on string or sewn on cloth, one by one. Shell decorations are usually grouped into linear patterns or geometric shapes.

TRY IT

Just try it as it is, inventing your own design. Bead stringing is so universal that methods of doing it are essentially the same all over the world.

A Kamba necklace, called *ngewa*, worn by married women for dancing. The core is made from the flexible roots of the Muaa tree, which are collected and shaped by male craftsmen. The women who wear these necklaces thread these trade beads onto a sisal thread and coil them spirally around the root.

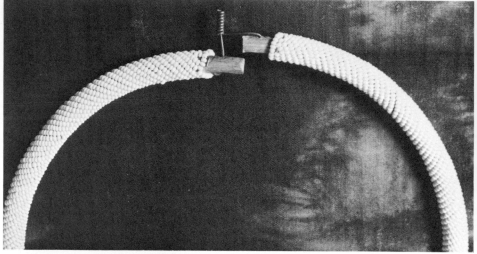

Note the clever wire closing. A coil of wire slips off a straight projection of wire.

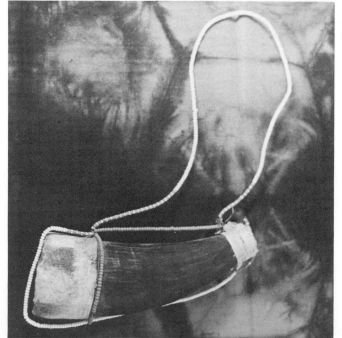

An old man's snuffbox called *ikutu*, from the Kamba tribe, made of Doum Palm (*Ilala*) mounted on cowhorn. Bead decorations and neck hanging strap are strung on wire.

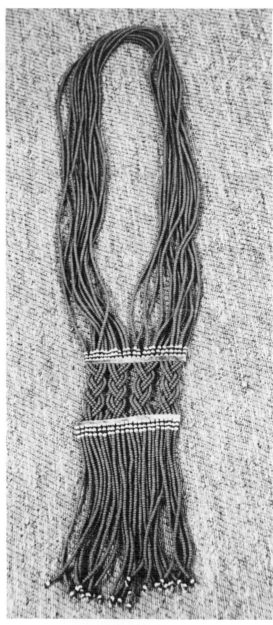

A Turkana bead necklace of fourteen strands strung on fiber by Turkana girls and young married women for everyday wear. Several of these heavy necklaces may be worn together.

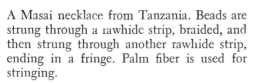

A Masai necklace from Tanzania. Beads are strung through a rawhide strip, braided, and then strung through another rawhide strip, ending in a fringe. Palm fiber is used for stringing.

An oil painting with beads adhered via epoxy by Jimoh Buraimoh of Oshogbo, Nigeria.

Also pp. 21 & colored plages preceding p. 19

Another painting by Buraimoh. The base is plywood.

7

∧∧∧∧∧∧∧∧∧∧∧∧∧

WORKING
WITH
METALS

∨∨∨∨∨∨∨∨∨∨∨∨

To the African working with metals, such as in casting bronze and forging iron, it was a mystical and poetic experience. The processes themselves with all their metallurgical difficulties, sensed but not understood, were magical. Bits of metal were fused into life with fire. And fire was fearsome as well as beneficent because it could destroy as well as create. Many taboos and ceremonies were connected with these processes. Taboos were observed as much to ensure success as to maintain time-honored secrets.

∧∧∧
HISTORY

The secret of making bronze was said to have traveled from the Near East, Asia Minor, through the north of Africa along the trans-

Saharan trade route system and was practiced as early as 2500 B.C. There is evidence of similarities in design and process among Greek, Arabic, Spanish, and Ethiopian as well as in Western Sudan and East African designs. These bronze pieces appeared very early in the picture.

Smelting iron was known in Africa from the first millennium B.C. In 400 B.C., iron smelting was introduced to the kingdom of Napata in West Africa. Iron was also found in the Nok culture of northern Nigeria. (Meroë was one of the earliest centers of the art.)

Iron and bronze were not the only forms of metalworking. Copper was widely used, as well as gold and silver. Gold, in fact, became a medium of exchange of the divine kings. The gold-salt trade helped create very powerful kingdoms. The Ashanti kingdom was one. All Ashanti gold belonged to the king, who represented the nation. Even though commoners could use gold, it was held in trust just for use in trading. Ashanti gold weights, used to weigh gold, symbolized the presence of the king, his omnipresence and omnipotence as the agent of the ultimate authority in the heavens. People used these small brass weights to weigh out gold. They were small, flat blocks, with top surfaces decorated in high relief, or were miniature sculptured forms representing a proverb or figure of speech. After a while, these pieces became just a symbol and were not used much. Priests wore gold soul disks called *akrafo-konmu* as a badge of responsibility. It was the priest's responsibility to maintain the purity of the king's soul. As the king's soul went, so did the condition of the country.

Gold was to some African countries a medium of exchange. The barter system served most areas for exchanges in everyday living. Cowrie shells also were a universal form of money. But some kingdoms developed still other forms. In Islamic countries, gold was prohibited by the Prophet so silver was used, particularly silver coins. African slave merchants priced their human parcels in bars of iron. At one point each bar of iron was equivalent to two shillings. Gold to some Africans was synonymous with the sun and king, reflecting the light and life of the nation. Silver was the color of moonlight and represented the queen and moon as well.

As civilization evolved, so did refinement of the metalworking arts. The art of bronze casting, employing the lost-wax process (cire perdue), flourished in the old kingdoms of Ife and Benin, as well as in many other parts of Africa. Most of the subjects of bronze casting were closely connected to court life with the forming of ritual objects and flat panels for palace walls. A rare example of realism in African art appeared in the sculptured portraits of Benin royalty and in the representation of courtly scenes.

The art of bronze casting flourished in the old kingdoms of Ife and Benin, but existed in many other parts of Africa. This brass collar is from the Bateke people of the Congo. Engraving and punching of circular indentations is done after filing and sanding of the piece.

/.V.\
OBJECTS OF METAL

In the Ivory Coast, gold was symbolized in all mythological tales and legends as a sacred heritage under control of earth spirits. Some, like the Baulé, used it for decoration as well.

All over Africa, jewelry, whether metal, shell, or bead, was a valued object and was worn as a badge of distinction. Metal found its way as ornamentation into a wide range of uses—as earrings and earplugs, labrets, nose ornaments, hairpins, necklaces, bracelets, anklets, rings, combs, and as trimming for sandals. Breastplates, belts, and sheaths for weapons were also made of metal. Tutsi chiefs used wood and metal wrist protectors in archery. Masai women wore coiled wire around wrists, arms, and lower legs. Gold thread was woven into the Kente cloth of Ashanti kings. Ibo smiths (of Nigeria) made gates of iron, notably, the Awka gates. Ceremonial axes and throwing knives of iron and steel (sometimes inlaid with silver) were powerful weapons to most African tribes. The Dogon and Bambara of Mali ritualized the use of metal in agricultural tools and weapons by using symbols representing humans on these pieces. They also fashioned human figures from a single piece of iron and placed them on graves and altars.

Noteworthy among the Ashanti ceremonial pieces was the *kuduo*, a tall many-sided vessel with a flat or slightly rounded cover and circular base, decorated in relief or incised design and formed in the lost-wax process. Used in purification rites, it was filled with gold dust and other vital ingredients and was buried with the dead. These were discovered in the mausoleums of Ashanti kings in Bantama near Kumasi. Other gold objects were melted down and destroyed because the art form was not considered so important as the worth of the gold.

/.V.\
PROCESS

Some people valued iron, bronze, and brass as highly as gold (perhaps because the flow of gold was controlled by kings). Smiths became powerful people belonging to closed guilds. They were so powerful in some tribes that they could cross tribal lines, marry royalty, and even rule as kings. The smithy became a center, a gathering place for men, as long as they followed the rules—and there were many because mysticism was strong. The smith's realm was a powerful one. Fugitives, even, could find sanctuary in the smithy, just as Christians could in a church. Indeed, the smith provided many vital needs of society. Agricultural implements would succeed in producing bountiful crops, if the smith invoked that magic in forming the tool; and weapons could prove a man's bravery, if the smith provided those magical attributes.

The smith deserved his place in society, for his art symbolized a highly developed technology, high on the scale of human accomplishment. Finding and refining ore was one accomplishment. But cooking iron from crumbs of ore into pig iron is a complex process. For instance, if too much oxygen is introduced into the furnace, and too little carbon monoxide is present, iron will reoxidize and the process can be a failure. Indeed, iron ore with too much phosphorus or other minerals can result in a very poor product. Modifying iron into steel by allowing wrought iron to absorb carbon slowly is another art that takes hours. Then after four-sided iron bars are formed, objects are forged, while red hot, by pounding the ingot with skillful, forceful blows with hammer on an anvil. No wonder the smith achieved his exalted status!

Masters of the lost-wax process in bronze and brass casting were also considered very important people. Indeed, kings sought to capture and lure bronze casters to their tribes. If one was captured and could prove his skill, he was given his freedom.

The lost-wax process varied somewhat from tribe to tribe. Basically, it involves forming an object from wild beeswax. As honey flows out from the combs, wax is pulverized in a mortar and boiled in water. Then the wax is skimmed off and filtered through a cloth in cold water. As the wax hardens on the bottom, it forms into flat cakes the shape of the container bottom.

Before forming cakes of wax into objects, wax is allowed to soften in the sun. Modeling, rolling and coiling, carving and incising are some ways wax is shaped. After achieving a form, sprues shaped like rods, often with solid funnel-shaped ends, are attached (to permit melted wax and air to flow out of one sprue, while molten metal enters the other sprue). Then the wax is encased in clay—clay and charcoal for fine work, or clay and dung for coarser work.

If work is finely detailed, it is covered with two parts of finely pulverized charcoal mixed into a thin paste with one part water. It is applied with a chicken feather (in lieu of a brush). When the first layer dries, another coating is applied until the charcoal is about as thick as an eggshell. Then clay and dried dung are mixed together in equal parts and the hole is covered, leaving small openings where the wax sprues reach the surface.

Then an assortment of metal scraps (screws, wire, battery parts, and other castaway pieces) are placed in a crucible and positioned upside down over the sprue holes. Then more clay-dung is applied to attach it to the base containing the wax form. Next the unit is placed over a piece of clay (that has holes in it, looking much like a frog for arranging flowers). The furnace is a cylindrical baked clay form with a hole at the bottom through which air from a bellows is pumped.

Variations occur in the kinds of bellows used, which may be merely the pumping of a piece of leather up and down over a pipelike form, or the traditional accordionlike bellows form of leather and wood. Also, the Tuaregs, Krans, Dans, Hausas, and Dini pour molten metal from a crucible into the form from which wax has been melted. The Ashanti, Akan, Baulé, Bamum, however, use the smelting crucible that just was described.

Meanwhile, charcoal, which starts burning with the aid of twigs and grass, has been heating in the furnace, as air pumped from the bellows intensifies the heat. After about a half hour, tongs are used to reverse the position of the mold; the sundry bits of metal have become molten and pour into the cavity left by wax that has long before vaporized out of the mold.

With tongs, the mold is lifted from the furnace and in a few more seconds, dunked into water. The clay-dung nearly falls apart revealing the new bronze form that has taken the place of the wax. But it needs refinement. A file is used to clean away particles and scale. Sometimes though, for fine work, potash is rubbed over the surface to sand the metal clean.

Most metals can be shaped by cold hammering and with periodic annealing (use of heat). This is the case with copper, aluminum, and bronze. But iron can only be formed or forged when red hot.

Bronze is employed in most areas of Africa, but brass was used along the coastal area of Guinea. The mixture contained little tin and more zinc than lead. Today, with the use of sundry scraps of metal, whether a piece is bronze or brass may vary from casting to casting.

Other metal processes are used. Silver coins, usually silver Maria Theresa thalers, are hammered out and drawn into wire. Solid casting requiring the pouring of metal into a scooped-out clay or sandy soil mold is another method. Aluminum, from pots and pans, is melted and then, when cooled, pounded and beaten into new shapes and then hammered and engraved. Copper is also formed with hammer and heat. Embossing, punching, engraving, incising, and polishing are accomplished with a wide range of whatever is available to mark and inscribe the metal surfaces. The damascening of iron and the inlaying of silver, gold, copper, and brass, and braided wire have also been part of the African's accomplishment with metals.

MAKING A BRACELET IN THE LOST-WAX PROCESS IN BOLGATANGA, GHANA

Scrap wire in copper and brass untwisted in the first step in making a bracelet.

After several strands have been dissembled from various sources, they are placed in a homemade . . .

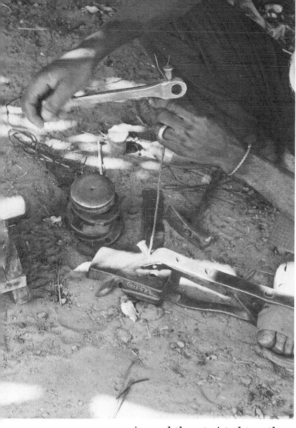

. . . vise and then twisted together.

After twisting, the wire is pounded flat with an improvised hammer.

And then, in the homemade vise, bent and hammered into a curved bracelet shape.

Beeswax is softened and rolled into a pencil-thick piece.

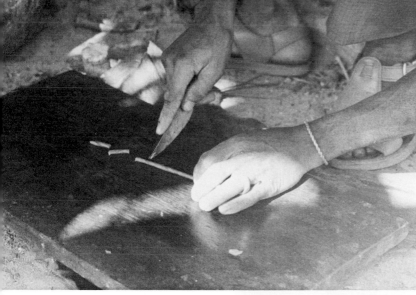

Inch-long pieces are cut from the wax coil . . .

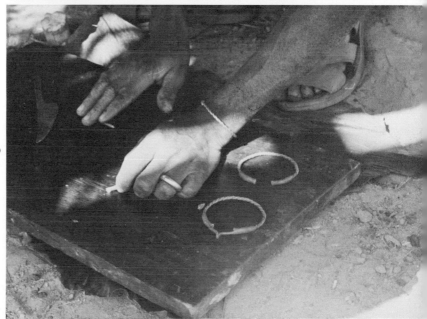

. . . and attached to the raw ends of the wire. He then molds the wax into the shape that he would like the finished piece to be.

Additional wax is rolled into a thinner diameter.

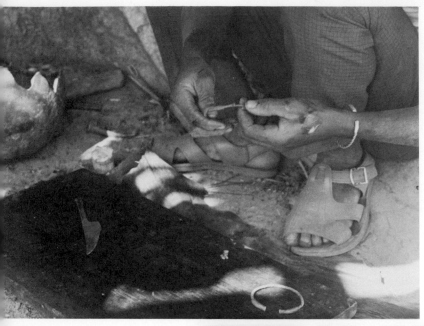

And pieces are attached to the ends and joined so that a bridge of wax is formed, as seen clearly in the previous photo.

Now investment material is being prepared. Dried dung is added to the clay—about half and half.

Both are kneaded together with a bit of water, to mix the materials into a moldable, plastic composition.

This mixture is then rolled out into a thick coil . . .

. . . and the bracelet is buried in the clay. Three bracelets are covered with the clay dung investment material this way.

The three are combined then, all with sprue points, slightly uncovered at their tips, facing the same way.

Into a pancake of investment material that has been formed in a bowllike shape, called the crucible, scraps of bronze and brass are added.

With sprue parts down, the crucible is attached to it with a bit more clay. The wet clay-dung investment is now ready to be placed in the furnace.

A clay form, with holes that make it look much like a frog used in flower arranging, rests over a hole that leads to the bellows. Air will be pumped through those holes to intensify the fire and increase its temperature.

Straw and charcoal are used to fuel the fire. A covering of straw is layered in the base of the furnace.

The invested wax and metal bracelets are placed on the bed of straw . . .

. . . and more straw and charcoal are placed in the furnace.

The fire is lighted. Bellows, made by pumping a sheet of leather up and down over a pipelike form, is pumped to add oxygen to the flame.

After firing for twenty minutes, the investment is lifted from the furnace with crucibles, and turned upside down so that the melted metal could flow into the cavity left by the evaporated beeswax.

After a few minutes, the piece is dunked into water and the investment starts to break apart.

The bracelets, at this point, are red hot. After cooling a while, they are placed in water and then the finishing process can begin.

The now unnecessary sprues are cut away with an improvised chisel.

Rough edges are filed smooth.

The result is handsome, but edges of bronze are somewhat rough because speed, rather than workmanship, is more important. The ends of the bracelet worn by the craftsman, however, were very finely finished.

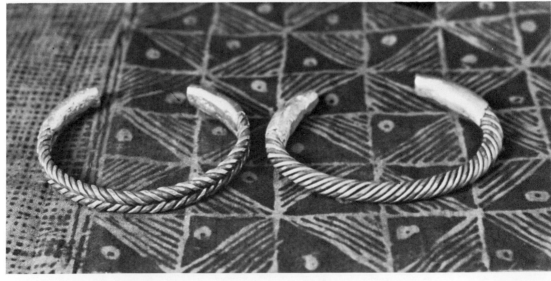

Two other bangles done in the lost-wax casting process. The bracelet on the left is from Kano, Nigeria. Decorative notches are cut into the spiral design. The meaning of the hanging charms has been lost. The bracelet on the right is from Upper Volta; its design seems to be derived from forged examples where a bar of metal is twisted and knotted. These bracelets are associated sometimes with healing rituals.

Unlike most African art, these brass figures from Dahomey have no particular religious or ceremonial purpose. Made in the lost-wax process, these contemporary three-dimensional scenes from Dahomey pictorialize some aspects of their life-styles. Here the king is sitting in his boat smoking a long pipe while one of his attendants fans him. Other figures are fishing or rowing (their oars are missing).

TRY IT

The lost-wax process is a universal skill independently developed by peoples in different parts of the world. Wax is easy to get and work. Small kits also are available so that the hobbyist can employ the lost-wax process in studio or kitchen. It requires investing the wax form in a plasterlike material and then using the equipment. With some practice, results can be gratifying.

It is also possible to mold a form of wax and then to take it to a caster who works for the jewelry trade. These professionals will invest your form into a mold and cast it in silver, gold, or whatever you wish. You then will need to file, clean, and polish your creation.

On the left is a nose pendant that goes through a pierced nasal septum and hangs over the lips. It is worn by elders of various tribes on ceremonial occasions. From the Turkana of Kenya, it is shaped by cutting and beating aluminum. Similar forms are found in Uganda, as well.

On the right is a *kome*, a Borana aluminum anklet worn by married women of the Borana and Gabbia tribes. They are made by Konson (Kenya) blacksmiths from melted-down cooking pots (called *sufurias*) and then, after forging, decorated with a small awl.

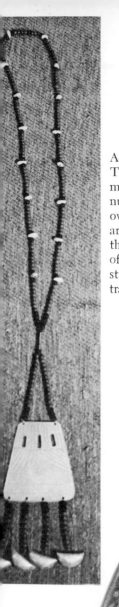

A Kamba (Kenya) necklace called *nzili*. They are worn by men as well as young married women for special dances. Aluminum pendants are decorated with a small owl and the small crescent-shaped bells are filled with small stones or seeds so that a tinkling sound adds to the music of the dance ceremony. Cowrie shells are strung, at intervals, between red and blue trade beads.

A copper tray made by heating and hammering copper. The designs are made by hitting an awl or nail with a hammer (punching) on the copper. Speck by speck the design emerges. From Kano, Nigeria.

Contemporary aluminum répoussé panels depicting scenes from Yoruba life by Asiru Olatunde of Oshogbo, Nigeria. They are made by pressing out figures from the back of the aluminum and defining and inscribing details around and on figures with an awl and hammer from the front.

8

MMMMMMMMMM

CARVING
WOOD
AND IVORY

VVVVVVVVVVVVV

There are many excellent sources describing all aspects of African wood carving (more thoroughly than covered here), because as an art form, wood carving is indigenous to all parts of Africa, and has received early notoriety. But *not* to include a reference to carving, particularly with wood, would be to omit a very important art and craft form.

MM

KINDS OF CARVINGS

The best-known wood carvings are masks and sculptures. They have proliferated throughout the centuries and fill collections in museums and galleries. There are, however, many other carved wooden forms that serve useful and decorative functions all over Africa. Doors are carved; large trees are hollowed out to form grain mortars, drums, and canoes. There are wooden pestles, beer troughs, handles and shafts, bark, beaters, zithers, and other musical instruments, walking sticks, dishes, plates and cups, stools, knife sheaths, dog and cow bells, vases and wooden pots, honey barrels, beehives, weaving bobbins, fly brushes, spoons, and combs. (I doubt whether this list is complete.) All are carefully hand carved according to tradition and need; and all are hand finished, and sometimes decorated. Size varies greatly from canoes to combs. Masks, and sculptures too, may vary from huge pieces six to eight feet tall to small delicate ancestor figures and small finely carved masks.

Masks, as we see them, attached to a wall, or as solo performers in a photo, are not complete. They really belong to a costume and are associated with a particular role in a particular ceremony. The size and shape of a mask, and all its attachments, are given meaning through movement and rhythm, and the mood of the ceremony. Seeing a mask without its costume and without its role in a ceremony is like seeing a stage set without a play.

Large trees are hollowed out to form canoes. This scene is from Ganvie, Dahomey. (These same canoes are made today by bush Negroes in Surinam and Guyana, South America.)

Long drums such as this one by the woodworkers of Busoga, Uganda (the Bugandas, too), are hollowed out from a soft wood and covered with python skin. Heights vary from twelve inches to thirty-six inches.

Grain mortars and beer troughs are also hollowed out from large pieces of wood. This Himba (Southwest Africa) wooden vessel is about twelve inches tall.

Finely carved and detailed Yoruba box and stool.

Carved hardwood stool from Korhogo, Ivory Coast.

Top view of the Korhogo stool.

The large cowbell carved from a single piece of hardwood is from Ethiopia. At lower left is a wooden-handled knife from Uganda.

A weaving bobbin from northern Ivory Coast or Mali.

Assorted carved hardwood forms. Top two right: knife sheaths from the Congo. The two left top forms are fetish figures. The one on the far left is by the Mayombe, and the one to the right of it is by the Kabre. Center is a Mayombe musical instrument. At the bottom, second from the left, is a Zulu cane; the combs are from the upper Ivory Coast.

A wooden bracelet with metal inlay applied
while in a molten state by the Watussi from
Ngozi Province, Burundi. *Courtesy: Smithsonian Institution*

A pipe for the smoking of marijuana by the Pygmies of the Congo-Uganda border.

There are masks that are worn like helmets, others that are headdress types as well as those that rest on the shoulders or cover the face. The Senufo have a mask for two. The huge Nimba masks of Baga, French Guinea, are borne by the shoulders. These masks move slowly through the crowd and sway side to side. Smaller forms go swirling around and relate to different movements, all orchestrated to some particular ceremony.

A Makonde (Bantu) ceremonial mask of softwood, painted black and hollowed out to fit over the head. Real hair is adhered to the top, beads hang from the ears, and a disk from the cork of a champagne bottle adorns the upper lip. The face is scarred with tribal lines.

Similar to the Pwevo mask (of the Lwenga tribe, Angola) this Nalindelle mask could also represent woman, a symbol of the source of life, the creator of abundance. The finely carved and marked wooden face is attached to a basket frame upon which a sisal hair cap is woven. Its fierceness suggests initiation purposes.

This limban sculpture by the Bambara people is so large that it could fit over the shoulders. But in actuality it is a fishing fetish that is placed on the beach when fishermen go out to fish, to look over them.

Typical of ceremonial masks is this example of a symmetrical piece from the Senufo.

The Dogon mask from Mali fits over the face.

A very large head mask from the Grunshi Kudugou area in Upper Volta. The mask is of softwood, colored with kaolin and terra-cotta, with areas of darkened wood exposed.

Another Makonde mask that depicts the devil.

A five-foot mask that fits over the head, complete with fiber head covering to hide the wearer's identity. From Upper Volta, it is used in funeral and agricultural rites.

Palm fibers, used as hair and dress, hemp, real hair, raffia, and leather, are made into fringes or layers to cover the body. Sometimes the costume is accompanied by a coarsely woven fiber cloth, a netlike fabric or bark cloth sewn to a wicker frame to cover the body. This helps to hide the identity of the wearer and serves to create a psychological as well as a physical relationship between the wearer and the mask.

Nearly all masks are connected in some way to initiation or fertility rites or to ancestor cult ceremonies of the poro-association. Masks have very long traditions that gave them meaning, but today this is beginning to fade away. They function as protectors during circumcision or initiation time; they maintain social order by dint of fear—generating a mystical significance. And they function as local entertainment in a positive, as well as negative (mischievous) sense. They also accompany groups to funerals, as do ancestor figures.

Ancestor figures complement the mask by becoming a channel through which one can speak to the ancestor because it symbolizes the ancestor's spirit (but is not a repository for the spirit).

Sculptures can be huge, medium-sized, or small memorials to the dead. Carvings are used on ritual posts, on chief's thrones, doorposts, lintels, and posts that hold up roofs. Elaborate carvings also are on the big drums that were kept in the center of villages to act as telegraph systems. These existed in West Africa long before the Europeans arrived on the scene.

The Baulé call their commemorative statues *waka sona*, meaning wooden people or figures. Some of these subjects come from legend and fable, others are zoomorphic effigies. *Ndiadan* for chief, *aboya* for dwarf, are two of many functioning forms. *Ndiadan* is used for the male initiation cult, and *aboya* functions to distribute worldly goods, strength, fertility, as well as exorcism of the sick and satisfaction of occult revenge. He is a handy fellow.

The Senufo ceremonial stick called *tefolopitian*, or *daleu*, is topped with a carving of a human figure, often female, and is used in poro ceremonies and on certain ritual or initiation occasions.

The Ghanaian Akan wooden seat, which also existed long before the Europeans came to Africa, functions as an actual seat, but also symbolizes the state of office of a chiefship. These Akan stools are sometimes blackened to commemorate the death of a favorite king. Blackening preserves the stool and the memory. It is of such importance to the Akan that without it the religion of ancestors becomes almost meaningless.

These are just a few of many hundreds of kinds, styles, and functions of various carved-wood forms.

A carved coconut head with shell teeth sits on a wooden body covered with a netted fiber costume. Attributed to the Congo area, perhaps Likasi.

A Baluba spirit figure.

An ancestor figure attributed to the Senufo. Note the tattoos.

A small (eight-inch) Senufo ancestor figure.

/∧∧\
DESIGN AND EXPRESSION

Since the carver creates these very important religious pieces, he usually (but not always) holds a very exalted place in a community, along with the blacksmith, who may also carve. Carving is a man's trade filled with ceremony. Trees are alive with spirits, and in order to appease the spirit of the tree before felling it, sacrifices of eggs, fowl, and sheep have to be made. The Akan may say, "Sɛsɛ tree, here is a chicken for you. I am going to fell you and make a stool out of you. Receive this offering and eat it. Please do not let the tool cut me. Do not let me suffer afterwards; and let me have a good price for the stool!"

Since the spirit of the tree is deprived of its home, it is likely to return on occasion to the object carved from that tree. So similar sacrifices have to be made to consecrate the completed stool, drum, or whatever has been carved. Sometimes blood of fowl or wine is poured over the piece and prayers are spoken. This is protection, but also helps give the raw wood a patina.

The wood carver deserves his status. He is a highly trained craftsman. He understands the characteristics of wood, use of tools, and the tribal stylistic language. Most important about the carver is the automatic, spontaneous, or instinctive way he expresses the spiritual aspects of his carving. The sculptor is obsessed with poetic and spiritual themes that have been imbued in him and embodied in generations of religious ceremony and folklore. That is the art of African wood carving, even though the same set of conventions are combined and recombined, resulting in products that look very similar. The sculptor is concerned with traditional as well as personal identity, as if he were an actor playing an old established role. He can carry it off as a profound expression or it could turn out to be fumbling and crude. Inspiration commands form; technique submits to the discipline of the medium.

African carvings usually are symmetrical and static. Those are the only two universals. Sometimes forms are naturalistic (as in Benin portrait sculptures), but most often they are conventionalized, stylized, and symbolized in a wide range of approaches. Some pieces look Cubist, others aggressive and brutal, assailing our senses with its impact. Masks of the forest dwellers, Guere, are regarded by Ivory Coast Africans as the most potent masks because of their direct assault on our senses. Power is implied by symbolism, by representing aspects of an elephant,

A very large (five-foot) ceremonial mask from Boko Nle, Upper Volta. Colors are terra-cotta, kaolin, and charcoal.

Another similar mask from Upper Volta.

leopard, crocodile, ram, buffalo, or antelope. Necks may be lengthened to indicate beauty, legs foreshortened to denote strength, torsos lengthened, buttocks made bigger in the female than the male, feet made flat for strength. The right hand in the male figure is bigger because it greets society (the left hand performs all unclean functions). Emphasis is on frontality. Decoration is almost always geometric.

Smaller pieces are usually carved from hardwood such as ebony and mahogany, and so-called steel woods. The bombax tree is most frequently used. But the iroko, makore, blablengole, and silk cotton tree are also choices. Softer woods usually are used for larger forms. Choice, however, is determined by the carver's locality, race, personality, and the nature and dimensions of the work. If a carver is going to carve a thick form, as the Senufo do in making a drum, a softer wood is used. But if a thinner, smaller form such as a mask by the Dan is the subject, then a hard wood would produce a better result.

Decorations usually are used on soft wood because surfaces are dull. They may be painted with any of the three most common colors— white, black, or terra-cotta. White comes from kaolin, black from charcoal, and terra-cotta from clay. Yellow is used less frequently on figures from Nigeria, the Cameroons, and Congo. Blue and green show up most often on forms from Dahomey and Southern Nigeria. Some pieces are decorated with inlays such as eyes of glass, ivory, or metal; cowrie shells stuck on with gum or beeswax, and vegetable fibers or real hair for head covering. Thin leaves of copper and silver (rarely gold) are hammered on occasionally. Bracelets, necklaces, earrings, headpieces of beads, stones, shells, bones, leather, horns, ivory inlays, animal tusks, nails, and seashells also honor the figure or mask.

Hardwoods take a polish well and often are rubbed with palm oil, several times during the two weeks that follow carving, mainly because work usually starts soon after felling the tree while the wood is in a green state when it is easier to work. The oil fills the pores causing the wood to cure more slowly. Soot, grease, sap from roots, and leaves are used to finish wood. Blackening occurs also with smoke and dust from the hut—and also with the sprinkling of libations of beer or blood. Occasionally, patterns are burned onto the surface. Camwood powder is used to keep termites from attacking the wood—a debilitating problem in Africa.

ᛉᛉᛉ

MAKONDE CARVING

There are exceptions to the usual stylistic rules of African carving. The Makonde, Bantu formerly from Mozambique, who live in Tanzania, also have a rich, long tradition and language of sculpture. It may have proved to be too active for them because the Makonde now create an art that still has roots in tradition, but is not traditional. There is a huge range of individuality, and yet some consistency without the need to use the same set of conventions as did their forefathers. Like the Eskimos, they only faintly echo historical heritage. What shows up is imagination, wit, and vitality. Each piece of wood suggests another image. Human form and movement are the consistencies that animate each creation. Birds, snakes, and beasts embody human form, man, and add their symbolic power to him. And like their African peers, their carving is monoxylous, made out of a single piece of wood, usually ebony and, occasionally, ivory.

Trees of hardwood, such as ebony, are sold by the government of Tanzania to sculptors so that forests can be preserved. No sculptor in Tanzania is allowed to chop down his own trees.

A cooperative of Makonde carvers near Arusha, Tanzania.

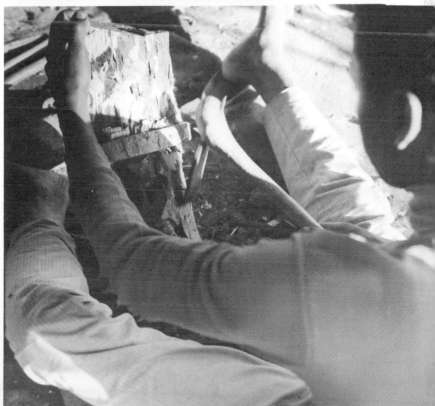

A piece of wood is blocked out with an adz.

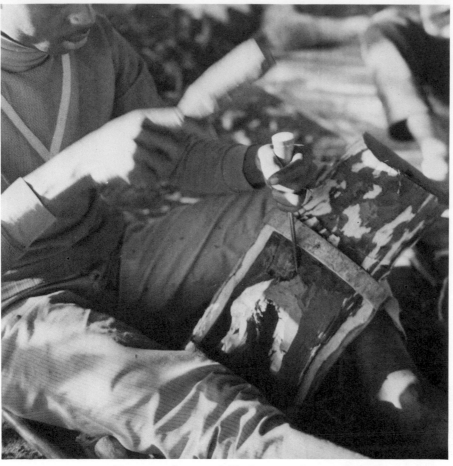

For areas that are difficult to reach, a mallet and chisel may be used.

Refinements are made with smaller adzes until the figure is nearly completed.

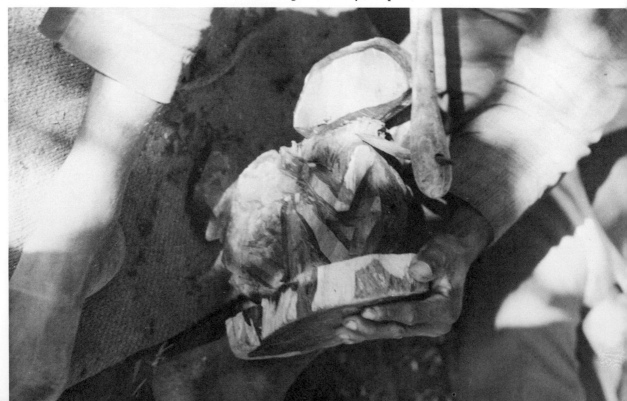

Finishing is accomplished with a knife and further refined with sanding.

Two views of a Makonde sculpture that depicts two scenes on each of four sides.

A bas-relief that satirizes the mask form. The outside stripes of light-colored wood are the outside layer, the way the natural wood looks.

Two views of a five-foot sculpture in which figures, totem fashion, sit over figures.

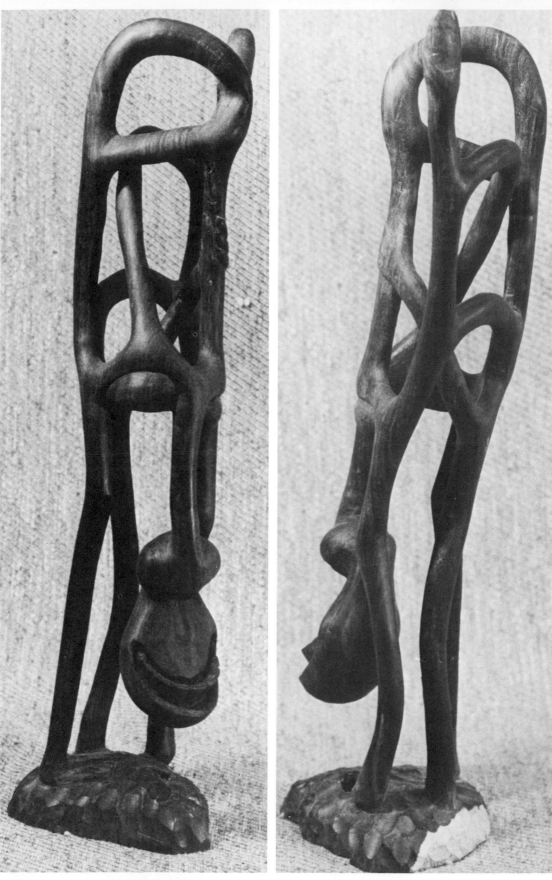

Two views of an abstract Makonde sculpture. Parts of the human form are enlarged, elongated, and decreased. A fingernail may be as long as a finger.

Another abstract Makonde sculpture showing two views.

Makonde sculptures vary with each sculptor. This one is solid, with figures emerging out of other figures, whereas others may be very elongated.

⋀⋅⋀⋅⋀
THORN CARVING

Another exception in African carving is the recent (since the 1930s) thorn carvings of Owo, Nigeria. Large thorns of several kinds and colors from the *ata* and *egun egun* trees, with the finest coming from Shagamu, are used. They are three colors—cream, rose (*egun egun*), and brown. Thorns may vary in size from small pieces the size of a fingernail up to four to five inches high and two to three inches thick. They are comparatively soft and are easily carved. Different colors are used for one piece. No finishing is necessary.

Thorn carving started as stamps to identify books and papers and evolved into miniature folk art pieces depicting aspects of Nigerian life.

THORN CARVING FROM OWO, NIGERIA

Thorns from various parts of Nigeria in three colors—cream, rose, and brown.

Thorns are relatively soft and may be carved with a penknife.

Rice is cooked with water and then used as an adhesive when it has become a viscous paste. Ola Fesese is applying glue with a stick.

The arm is being held in place for a few moments until the glue begins to set.

A completed thorn carving.

All thorn carvings are miniatures that depict scenes from Nigerian life. This is a comment about the Nigerian war with the former state of Biafra.

More thorn-carved scenes from Nigerian life. These miniatures are a modern-day departure from traditional African carving, which is usually monoxylous, symmetrical, and symbolic.

/\./\.\ IVORY AND BONE CARVING

Ivory traditionally was considered a symbol of power. All ivory was given to the chief who then had a right to dispose of it. Rarely seen now, an elephant tusk was set up in the ground alongside a forest path to mark the grave of an old chief, notable, or priest.

Ghanaians were very skillful carvers of ivory. Their carvings were used as royal decorations. Ivory was carved into forms for many purposes. The oliphant was a hunting horn made of ivory. Men of the northern part of the Ivory Coast wore ivory bracelets. Ivory was carved into amulets, handles, jewelry, combs. Miniature ivory forms were worn by initiates and became decorations for wooden forms.

Because of the threat of extinction of the elephant, and the greedy poaching for their valuable tusks, African countries are trying to curb the use of tusks. Tanzania, for one, has placed a ban on use of ivory for this reason. As a result, ivory carving is becoming more rare.

An ivory carver in Mombasa, Kenya. A knife is the principal instrument.

A miniature head carved by Makonde.

A carved elephant tusk from the Gabon River region of Gabon.

Another Makonde carving.

Work of a Makonde apprentice—a bas-relief on ivory.

⋀⋀⋀
PROCESS

Since most African carvings are monoxylous, the carver starts with a block of wood, and what finally emerges, without any gluing or attaching, is the completed form. The carver's tools are simple and few. Basically, he uses several sizes of adzes and a small knife. Sometimes a chisel and hammer are utilized, and a hook-shaped knife is used to hollow out small concavities such as spoons or the back of masks. Occasionally a hot poker burns holes or is used to reach hard-to-carve areas such as the underarms, and sometimes a flat piece of metal that acts like a carpenter's plane smooths the surfaces.

Measurements are made by handspan. A large adze chips away excess, blocking out areas until the form takes a rough shape. Then, with a series of smaller adzes, the carver skillfully and accurately chips away grooves for eyes, deepens cheeks, cuts under the nose and mouth—making small refinements to the whole piece continually working around the whole form. The adze is used almost until the piece is finished before a knife is called into service. Finer detail is carved with a knife. For final refinement, rough leaves are used to sand areas smooth and the piece is ready for finishing.

Carving elsewhere in Africa—other than the Makonde—is still very much the same. The adz is used to block out forms. Smaller adzes are used as more refinement is necessary. This is a carver from Ghana.

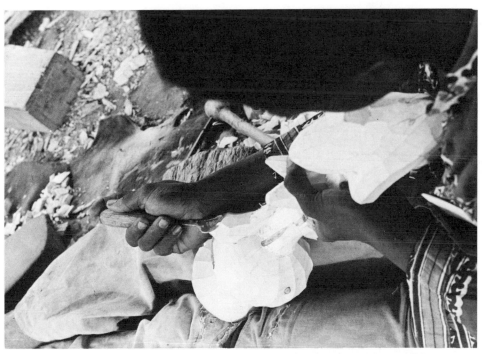

A spoon-shaped knife is used to scoop out areas and carve concavities. This carver is from the upper Ivory Coast.

A knife is also used to cut away smaller amounts of wood.

A large form that is nearly completed, in the foreground, along with an assortment of adzes.

Today most sculpture in Africa is either religiously following traditional rules, without embodying much of the traditional spirit, or it has departed from tradition in style, without completely leaving behind tribal heritage. The small seated figure, in hardwood, is a witch doctor, according to the stripes on his cheeks. It is obvious from tool marks that adz and chisel were the only tools employed. Both figures are from Nigeria.

TRY IT

Sculptures can be made without a vise, electric saws, drills, wheels, and elaborate chisel sets. Try simple tools and working with a block of "green" wood. Then use oil stains to seal the pores as the Africans do. Finishing and sealing can be accomplished in one step. Try crude oil, which is a dark brown, or Miniwax oil stains.

BIBLIOGRAPHY

∧∧∧∧∧∧∧∧∧∧∧∧∧
˙.˙˙.˙˙.˙˙.˙˙.˙˙.˙˙.˙˙

African Arts Magazine—all issues. Los Angeles, California: African Studies Center, University of California.

Bascom, William R. *The Yoruba of Southwestern Nigeria.* New York: Holt, Rinehart & Winston, 1969.

Beier, Ulli. *Contemporary Art in Africa.* New York: Frederick A. Praeger, 1968.

Boas, Franz. *Primitive Art.* New York: Dover, 1935.

Bossert, Helmuth. *Old Art of Asia, Africa, and the Americas.* New York: Frederick A. Praeger, 1964.

Chase, Judith Wragg. *Afro-American Art and Craft.* New York: Van Nostrand Reinhold, 1971.

D'Amato, Janet and Alex. *African Crafts for You to Make.* New York: Julian Messner, 1971.

Erikson, Joan Mowat. *The Universal Bead.* New York: W. W. Norton & Co., Inc., 1969.

Fagg, William, and Picton, John. *The Potter's Art in Africa.* London: The Trustees of the British Museum, 1970.

Figurative Art—Occasional Papers 1–5. Accra, Ghana: The National Museum of Ghana, 1970.

Gardi, René. *African Crafts and Craftsmen.* New York: Van Nostrand Reinhold Co., 1969.

GLUBOK, SHIRLEY. *The Art of Africa*. New York: Harper & Row, Publishers, 1965.

HODGES, HENRY. *Artifacts*. London: John Baker, 1971.

HOLAS, B. *Craft and Culture in the Ivory Coast*. Republic of the Ivory Coast, Ministry of Culture, 1968.

Horizon History of Africa, The. New York: American Heritage Publishing Co., Inc., 1971.

KOFI, VINCENT AKWETE. *Sculpture in Ghana*. Accra, Ghana: Ghana Information Services, 1964.

LEUZINGER, ELSY. *The Art of Africa*. New York: W. W. Norton & Co., Inc., 1969.

———. *The Art of Black Africa*. New York: Graphic Society, Ltd., 1972.

MEAD, MARGARET; BIRD, JUNIUS B.; and HINNELHEBER, HANS. *Technique and Personality*. New York: The Museum of Primitive Art, 1963.

MURPHY, E. JEFFERSON. *History of African Civilization*. New York: Thomas Y. Crowell Co., 1972.

OLDEROGGE, DMITRY, and FORMAN, WERNER. *Negro Art: The Art of Africa*. London: Paul Hamlyn, 1965.

O'SHAUGHNESSY, MARJORIE. *Basketry*. New York: Dover Publications, 1952.

RATTRAY, R. S. *Religion and Art in Ashanti*. London: Oxford University Press, 1969.

SARPONG, PETER. *The Sacred Stools of the Akan*. Tema, Ghana: Ghana Publishing Corp., 1971.

SIEBER, ROY. *African Textiles and Decorative Arts*. New York: The Museum of Modern Art, 1972.

STOUT, ANTHONY. *Modern Makonde Sculpture*. Nairobi, Kenya: Kibo Art Gallery Publications, 1966.

TYRRELL, BARBARA. *Tribal Peoples of Southern Africa*. Cape Town: Gothic Printing Company, 1968.

Uganda Crafts. Kampala, Uganda. Department of Culture and Community Development, 1953.

WASSING, RENÉ A. *African Art*. New York: Harry N. Abrams, Inc., 1968.

WILLIAMS, GEOFFREY. *African Design from Traditional Sources*. New York: Dover Publications, 1971.

For additional information:

A bibliography of African resource books can be found in issues of *Africana Library Journal*, Africana Publishing Corporation, 101 Fifth Avenue, New York, New York, 10003.

MAP OF AFRICA

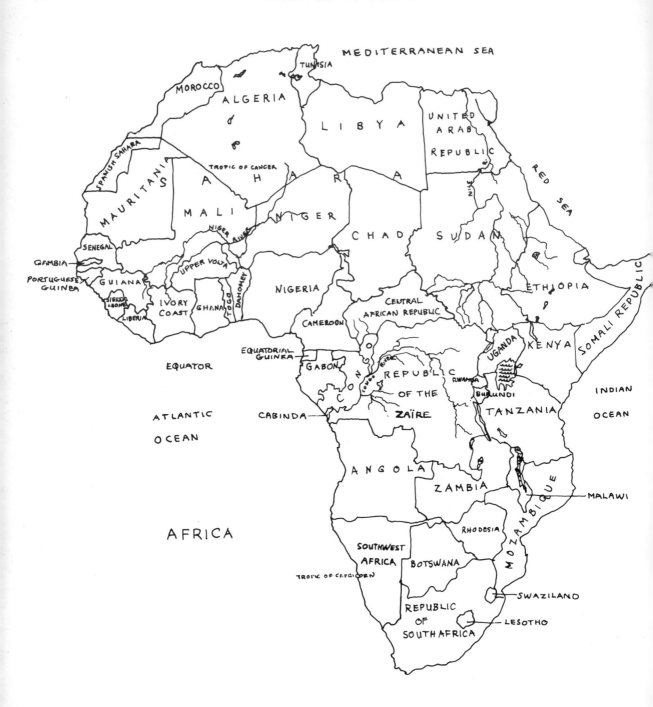

TRIBAL MAP

FEZZAN

SAHARA

FULANI

TUAREG
DOGON
TIMBUKTU BAMBARA SONGHAI MARABOUT
·AGADES

·DAKAR
KASONKE LAKE CHAD KORDOFAN
MANDINGO (FULANI) KURUMBA
BAGU FULBE HAUSA
·BOLGATANGA ·KANO WAYA
MENDE KORHOGO FRAFRA
KISSI SENUFO ·TAMALE ADDIS ABABA
DAN GURO KABRE
KRAN BAULÉ ·ABOMEY ·OSHOGBO
BETE ·OYO· IBO KOSO
KRU BAKIVE ASHANTI ·IBADAN YORUBA BAMUM
GA SHAI FON ·LAGOS BAMILEKE
ACCRA EKOI VAMBO

MANGBETU BORAN
GABBIA BORANA
TURKANA SUK SOMALI
ZANDE PYGMIES BUGANDA ABAGUSSI
WATUSSI POKOMO
BAKUBA LUVALE KIKUYU
KUBA LAKE ·NAIROBI·KAMBA
BUSHONGO VICTORIA WAKAMBA OR
BALUBA MASAI

KUBA BARUNDI MASAI ·MOMBASA
KASAI BASONGE BANTU
MAYOMBE LUBA MAKONDE

DAR ES SALAAM

LWENA

BANTU
MAKONDE
LAKE
NAYASA

KOTSE

BUSHMAN
THE
KALAHARI

TEMBU
JOHANNESBURG· SWAZI
NDEBELE
SOTHO
HIMBA ZULU

ZULU
CAPE TOWN

INDEX

Page numbers in *italics* refer to illustrations

A

Abagusii, the: millet beer pots (*ekei*) made by women of, 129, 166, *169*

Abomey, Dahomey: appliqué hangings from, 98–99

Accra, Ghana: woven bracelets from, *122*

Adinkra cloth, 79–89. *See also* Decoration of fabrics
  carved calabashes used as design stamps for, 79, 82, *84*
  patterns, 84–88
  preparing dye for, 79, 80–81
  steps in printing process, 82–84
  types of, 79

Adire eleko, 73, *73–78. See also* Decoration of fabrics
  patterns, *76, 77, 78*
  zinc stencils for, 73, *73, 74*

Adire eleso, 69, *69–71. See also* Decoration of fabrics
  patterns, *72*

Africa: people of, 14–15

African art
  changes in form of, 9–11, 13–14
  contemporary, 20–25
  kinds of, 16–17
  materials and tools for, 16
  qualities of, 2, 5
  variations in themes of, 9

African history, 11, 13–14

African trade beads, *212, 213*

Aggri beads, *193, 195*

Aluminum, 229, 230
  anklet worn by married women of Borana and Gabbia tribes, *242*
  contemporary repoussé panels by Asiru Olatunde of Oshogbo, Nigeria, *244*
  Kamba pendant worn on necklace (*nzili*), *243*
  nose pendant from Turkana of Kenya, *242*

Amber beads, Fulani, *199*

Ampoto, Oku: stone sculptures by, 22

Ancestor figures, *258, 260*

Appliqué
  on fabrics, 97, 98–101. *See also* Decoration of fabrics; Textile arts
  on leather, 186, *190*
  symbols used in, 97, 98–101

Art, African. *See* African art

Ashanti, the, 15
  Kente cloth of kings of, *62–63*, 227
  metal ceremonial piece (*kuduo*) of, *227*
  pottery-making by, 27
    in Pankronu, Ghana, 31, *41–48*, 49–51

B

Badee bark: preparation of, as dye for *adinkra*, 79, 80–81

Bakongo, the: pottery of, 27

Bakuba, the, 15
  pottery of, 27

Baluba, the: spirit figure carved by, *259*

Bambara, the, 15
  paintings on cotton cloth by, *63*. *See also* Decoration of fabrics
  use of metal by, 227
  wooden fishing fetish used by, *255*

Bamileke, the: raffia bags made by, *109*

Bantu tribes, 15

Bark cloth, 59
  carpet of, *60*
  kilt of, worn by Kuba kings, 61, *62*

Basketry, 127–46. *See also* Calabash
  construction techniques, *139, 140, 141*
    coiled basket, *139*
    twined basket, *139*
    wickerwork type, *139, 141*
  construction of Zaara basket, 130–36

as family affair by the Frafra of Korhogo, Ivory Coast, 128
materials for, 127, 128, 129
  preparation of, 129, 138
musical instrument made with straw and sealed with bottom of gourd, 139
tools for, 129
tray from Ruhengeri, Rwanda, 145
Baskets
  coiled:
    with decorative weaving in raffia, 145
    of grass bound with raffia, 143
    large hamper type, raffia wrapped, 144
    by Zulu, from Zululand, 146
  market for, in Korhogo, 137
  of raffia:
    decorated with cowrie shells, 196
    from Kano, Nigeria, 141
    from Sierra Leone, 142
  of straw, from Upper Volta, 142
  uses of, 129
Bast, 59
Batik, leather, 186. See also Decoration of fabrics: resist processes
Baulé, the: commemorative statues of, 258
Beads and beadwork
  African trade beads, 212, 213
  aggri beads, 193, 195
  amber beads, Fulani, 199
  bamboo-and-horn Swazi necklace, 213
  Bamum dolls decorated with beads and cowrie shells, 202
  bead ornament made in Nigeria, 217
  beadwork processes, 214, 214
    lazy stitching, 214, 219, 219
    materials for, 214, 215
    netted beadwork, 214, 218, 218
    for shells and bones, 219
    spot stitching, 217, 217
    woven beadwork, 214, 215, 215, 216
  belts made of cowrie shells, 195, 195
  bracelets made of beads lazy stitched on leather, 219
  Chiwamba dance form, 211
  on contemporary painting, 21, 222, 223

cowrie shells, 194, 195, 195, 196. See also Cowrie shells
fly whisk adorned with beaded handle, 201
of glossy straw, 199
hand-carved ivory beads on Bwamé bracelet, 212
history and background of, 193, 195
Kamba necklace (ngewa), with core made from roots of Muaa tree, 220
kinds of, 197, 212
on leather, 171, 172, 186, 210
linguist's staff from Nigeria, 201
of the Masai of East Africa, 203, 203–8, 213, 221. See also Masai, the
necklace of African trade beads, 213
necklace of bone and animal teeth, 198
ostrich shell beads, 195, 196
patterns of, 212
Pokomo necklaces, 215, 216
  kishinda, 215
reed necklace from Kenya, 197
shapes of beads, 212
sources of, 212
trade beads, African, 212, 213
Turkana necklace of fourteen strands, 221
Yoruba fan of ostrich feathers and beads, 200
of Zulus of South Africa, 4. See also Zulus, the
Belts
  of cowrie shells, 195
  leather, 188
Benin, Nigeria, 59
  leather fan from, 174
Bete, the: cowrie shell belts worn by, 195
Body decoration, 19, 195
Bolgatanga, Ghana
  bracelet made in, by lost-wax process, 230–40
  Frafra women preparing clay in, 28–29
  pots from, with incised designs, 54
  preparing and decorating calabashes in, 147, 149, 157–58
  woman's leather dress usually worn at "death" ceremony, 172
Borana, the: aluminum anklet worn by

married women of, 242

Bracelets. *See also* Beads and beadwork; Necklaces
of beads lazy stitched on leather, 219
of hand-carved ivory beads, 212
leather:
from Mali, 189
with painted designs, 191
uses of, 166–67
made by lost-wax process, 240, 241
steps in process, 230–40
nylon and polyethylene monofilament woven around metal bracelet blank, 122
wooden, with metal inlay, 252
of woven elephant hair, 146

Brass, 226, 227, 229
figures of, made by lost-wax process, 241

Bronze, 224–25, 229
casting of, using lost-wax process, 225–26

Buganda, the, 15
long drums made by, 247

Buraimoh, Jimoh: contemporary paintings by, 21, 222, 223

Burundi
large ceramic pot by Tutsi of, 57
wooden Tutsi bracelet with metal inlay from, 252

Bushmen, the, 14
cicatrization by, 19, 195
ostrich shell beads worn by, 195, 196

C

Calabash(es), 147–64. *See also* Basketry; Baskets
bowl and ladle, 159
carved, and used as *adinkra* design stamps, 79, 82, 84
decoration of, 148–49, 149, 150, 157–58
macramé cord design, 151
steps in carving, 148–49, 150
steps in scratching design, 157–58
tools for, 149
designs on, 152–56, 158–59, 160–63
regional, 149
gigantic carved calabashes from Iwo, Nigeria, 152, 154

Masai traveling container for blood and milk, 163, 203
preparation of, for use and decoration, 147
rattles, 161, 164
repairs to, 127
snuff bottle (*ikutu*) made from, 162
stringed instrument (*duuliga*) made from, 159
used as wall hanging when not in use, 156
uses of, 127, 147, 149

Cameroon
Bamum dolls decorated with beads and shells, 202
raffia bags made by the Bamileke of, 109

Canoes, 246

Carvings, 245–91
ancestor figures, 258, 260. *See also* Sculptures
canoes, 246
ivory and bone, 283, 283–85
kinds of, 245–46
masks. *See* Masks
process used for, 286, 286–90
tools, 286, 286, 287, 288, 289, 290
sculptures. *See* Makonde, the; Sculptures
symbolism of, 261, 263
thorn carving, 273, 273–82
of wood. *See* Wood carving

Cassava paste, 63, 73, 73, 74

Clay. *See* Pottery-making

Collars. *See* Necklaces and collars

Combs, carved, 251

Congo
cowrie shell necklace and back ornament from, 194
hardwood knife sheaths from, 251
Yaka: raffia cloth garment from, 109

Containers. *See* Basketry; Baskets; Calabash

Copper, 225, 229, 230
tray of, made by heating and hammering, 243

Cotton, 59
cleaning and spinning of, 102–3, 103–5

Cowrie shells, 195
attached to raffia basket, 196
belts of, for war dances and period

of tribal initiation, 195, *195*
combined with leopard teeth, as necklace and back ornament, *194*
dolls decorated with beads, seeds, and, *202*
on Kamba necklace with aluminum pendant, *243*
religious significance of, 195

D

Dahomey
  Abomey: appliqué hangings from, 98–99
  brass figures from, made by lost-wax process, *241*
  river people from along coastal waterways of, 6
Damsika, man's, *123*, *124*
Decoration, body, 19, 195
Decoration of fabrics, 61–101. *See also* Textile arts
  appliqué, 97, 98–101
    symbols used in, 97, 98–101
  painting on cotton cloth in style of the Senufos, 89–96
    designs, 89, 93–95
    preparing dye for, 89–90, *90*
    step in painting, 89–90, *91–93*
  printing process, *adinkra*, 79–89. *See also* Adinkra cloth
  resist processes, 66–78
    adire eleko, *73*, 73–78
    adire eleso, *69*, 69–72
    dyeing the fabric, *67*, 68
    patterns, 72, *76*, *77*, *78*
    plangi, 69
    preparing indigo dye for, 66–67, *67*
Decoration of leather, 174, 186
  appliqué, 186, *190*
  attaching ornaments, 184–85
  batik, 186
  beadwork, *171*, *172*, 186. *See also* Beads and beadwork
  designs, 179–80, *187*, *188*
  embroidery, *174*, *182–83*, *190*
  fringes, 186, *186–87*
  materials for, 186
  painting, 186, *187*, *191*
  woven leather strips, *169*, 186, *191*, *192*

Dodowa, Ghana: gold pin made in lost-wax process in, 23
Dogon, the
  mask from Mali made by, *256*
  straw beads worn by, 199
  use of metal by, 227
Dolls, 18
  decorated with beads and cowrie shells, *202*
  wooden, wearing leather toga, *171*
Dress, African, 19–20. *See also* Bracelets; Garments; Necklaces
Duuliga (instrument) made of calabash, *159*

E

Embroidery on leather, 174
  steps in process, 182–83

F

Fabrics
  decoration of. *See* Decoration of fabrics
  weaving of. *See* Weaving
Fakaha, Ivory Coast, xiv, 96
  cleaning and spinning of cotton in, 104–5
  printed textiles from, 93–95
Fans
  leather, *166*, *170*, *174*, *176*
  of ostrich feathers and beads, *200*
Feathers. *See* Ostrich feathers
Frafra, the
  basket made by, *138*
  basketry as family affair of, in Korhogo, Ivory Coast, 128
  preparing and decorating calabashes in Bolgatanga, Ghana, *147*, *149*
    scratching designs, 157–58
  women of, pounding dry clay into fine powder, *28–29*
Fulani, the, 15
  amber beads worn by, 199
  leather saddlebags made by, *166*, *168*
  man's leather hat, *174*
Fulbe, the
  calabash decoration by, *149*
  leatherwork of, *167*
    purse, using appliqué and embroidery, *190*

G

Ga, the, 15
  pottery-making by, in Weija (Ghana), 30–31, 32–38, 39, 39–40, 41
Gabbia, the aluminum anklet worn by married women of, 242
Garments. See also Belts; Bracelets; Necklaces; Purses; Saddlebags; Textile arts: garments
  Chiwamba beaded dance form worn by Matushi dancers, 211
  leather sandals, 167
  leather togas, and aprons or skirts, 166, 171, 172
    decorated with beads, 210
  man's leather hat formed over woven straw, 174
  woman's leather dress (vwuuo), 172
  Zulu beaded girdle, 211
Ghana
  Accra: woven bracelets from, 122
  Bolgatanga:
    bracelet made in, by lost-wax process, 230–40
    Frafra women preparing clay in, 28–29
    pots from, with incised designs, 54
    preparing and decorating calabashes in, 147, 149, 157–58
    woman's leather dress usually worn at "death" ceremony, 172
  center of Kente weaving in, 62
  Dodowa: gold pin made in lost-wax process in, 23
  Mampong-Akwapim: contemporary stone sculptures from, 22
  man's damsika made in, 123
  Pankronu: pots made in, from top down, 31, 41–48, 49–51
  Tamale:
    handwoven cotton from, 118
    leather bracelets from, 191
    village north of, 7
    weaving cooperative in, 111
  Weija: pots made in, from bottom up, 30–31, 32–38, 39, 39–40, 41
Gold, 225
  as medium of exchange of divine kings, 225
  pin made in lost-wax process, 23
  symbolism of, 227

H

Hairstyling, 19–20
  as art form in Korhoga, Ivory Coast, 8
Hamitic tribes, 15
Hassocks, leather, 181, 185
  steps in embroidering, 182–83
  steps in making, 178–81
Hausa, the, 12
  ceramic water bottle made by, 58
  leatherwork of, 167
    man's hat, 174
Haya, the: bark cloth carpet made by, 60
Himba, the: grain mortars and beer troughs made by, 247
History, African, 11, 13–14
Hlabisa near Nongoma, South Africa, 4

I

Ibadan, Nigeria
  embroidery on Yoruba man's gown from, 122
  hamper type basket from, 144
Ibo, the, 15
  red clay figure groups of, 27
  use of metal by, 227
Igbo-Ukwu, Nigeria, 59
Ikutu (snuff bottle)
  decorated with beadwork, 220
  made of calabash, 162
Indigo dye: preparation of, 66–67, 67. See also Decoration of fabrics
Instruments, musical. See Musical instruments
Ivory carving, 283, 283–85
Ivory Coast
  amber beads worn by Fulani of, 199
  boubou of damask cotton with batik pattern and machine embroidery, 125
  cowrie shell belts worn by the Bete of, 195
  Fakaha, xiv, 96
    cleaning and spinning cotton in, 104–5
    printed textiles from, 93–95
  hardwood combs from, 251
  Korhogo. See Korhogo, Ivory Coast
Iwo, Nigeria
  gigantic carved calabashes from, 152, 154–55

steps in calabash carving in, 148–49

J

Jewelry, 227. *See also* Bracelets; Necklaces
Johnson, E. Torto: gold pin made by, in lost-wax process, 23

K

Kabre, the: hardwood fetish figure of, 251
Kamba, the
  bead decorations on snuffbox made by, 220
  calabash snuff bottle made by, 162
  necklace (*nzili*) with aluminum pendant, 243
Kano, Nigeria
  bracelet made by lost-wax process in, 241
  calabash rattle made in, 161
  copper tray made in, 243
  raffia basket from, 141
Kente cloth, 62–63, 63, 64, 65, 227
Kenya
  Kamba calabash snuff bottle from, 162
  Kamba necklace (*nzili*) with aluminum pendant from, 243
  Masai beaded headdress from Mburu, 213
  Masai beaded necklaces and collars, 203, 203–4
  Masai lady's bead-decorated leather skirt, 171
  millet beer pots (*ekei*) made by Abagusii women of, 129, 166, 169
  Pokomo woven beaded necklaces from, 215, 216
  reed necklace from, 197
  Turkana aluminum nose pendant, 242
  Turkana ostrich shell beads, 196
  woven elephant hair bracelets from, 146
Kigezi, Uganda: basket from, with geometric pattern, 143
Korhogo, Ivory Coast
  basket market in, 137
  basketry as a family affair by the Frafra of, 128

bracelets of beads lazy stitched on leather, 219
hairdressing as art form in, 8
pottery-making in, 41, 55
village near, 6
weaver with loom, 120
woman's undergarment from, 122
Kuduo of the Ashanti, 227

L

Lafun, 73
Leather, 165–92
  bottles covered with, 169
  bracelets, 166–67, 189, 191
  briefcase with woven decoration from Mali, 192
  decoration of. See Decoration of leather
  embroidery on, 182–83
  fans, 166, 170, 174, 176
  feathers and, 176, 186
  grigris or *saphies*, 167, 173
  hassocks, 181, 185
  historical background, 165–66
  man's hat formed over woven straw, 174
  man's shoulder-strap purse, 186–87
  Masai headpiece of ostrich plumes attached to, 176
  millet beer pots (*ekei*), 129, 166, 169
  money purse with plastic weaving, 173
  perfume and cosmetic containers made of parchment covered with, 175
  pillow with transparent lacquerlike colors, 187
  preparation of skins and hides, 177
  tools and materials for, 177
  purses, 189, 190
  saddlebags, 166, 168
  sandals, 167
  shields, 166, 167
  storage container for sugar, 173
  Suk wig, to be worn around arm, made of ostrich feathers attached to, 176
  thonging, 179, 182
  togas and aprons or skirts, 166, 171, 172, 210
  tray with leather weaving, 191
  uses of 166–67, 167–76

working with, 177–78
    materials for, 178
    steps in making a hassock, 178–81
    tools for, 177
Leopard teeth: used as ornaments, 194, 198
Looms. *See* Weaving
Lost-wax process of casting, 228–29
    brass figures from Dahomey, 241
    bronze, 225–26
    gold pin made by, 23
    steps in making a bracelet, 230–40

M

Macramé cord design over calabash, 151
Makonde, the, 11, 15
    ceremonial masks of, 253, 257
    cooperative of carvers near Arusha, Tanzania, 265
    ivory carvings by, 284–85
    sculptures of, 264, 264–72
        finished pieces, 268–72
        steps in creation of, 265–68
        wood used in, 264, 264
Mali
    briefcase with woven decoration from, 192
    decorative Tuareg hanging ornaments from, 143
    Dogon mask from, 256
    straw beads worn in, 199
    stuffed leather bracelet from, 189
    Timbuktu:
        leather tray from, 191
        Tuareg container for storage of sugar, 173
        Tuareg man's shoulder-strap purse, 186–87
Mampong-Akwapim, Ghana: contemporary stone sculptures from, 22
Marabout, the: leatherwork of, 167
Masai, the, 11, 15
    beadwork of:
        headdress from Mburu, Kenya, 213
        necklace from Tanzania, 221
        necklaces and collars from Kenya, 203, 203–4
        women doing beadwork, 204–8
    calabash traveling container for blood and milk made by, 163

headpiece of ostrich plumes and leather made by, 176
    lady's leather skirt decorated with beads, 171
    leather shields made by, 166, 167
    Tanzanian woman leaning against dung-and-clay house, 7
    use of metal by, 227
Masks, 17, 21, 245, 246, 253, 258, 261
    decorations on, 258, 263
    Dogon mask from Mali, 256
    large head masks from Upper Volta, 256, 257, 262
    Makonde ceremonial masks, 253, 257
    Nalindelle mask, 254
    Senufo ceremonial mask, 255
    symbolism of, 258
    types of, 253
    use of, 18
Materials for art, 16
Mayombe, the
    hardwood fetish figure of, 251
    hardwood musical instrument of, 251
Metal and metalworking, 224–44
    aluminum, 229, 230
        anklet worn by married women of Borana and Gabbia tribes, 242
        contemporary repoussé panels by Asiru Olatunde of Oshogbo, Nigeria, 244
        nose pendant from Turkana of Kenya, 242
        bracelets done in lost-wax process, 240, 241
        brass collar from Bateke people of the Congo, 226
        brass figures from Dahomey, 241
        bronze, 224–25, 227, 229
        copper, 225, 229, 230
            tray made by heating and hammering, 243
        designs, 243
        gold, 225, 227
            pin, 23
        history of, 224–26
        iron, 225, 227
        processes of metalworking, 227–30
            cold hammering, 229
            lost-wax process. *See* Lost-wax

process of casting
 silver hammered out and drawn
  into wire, 229
 solid casting, 229–30
 uses of metal objects, 227
Millet beer pots (ekei) of leather and
 basketry, 129, 166, 169
Mombasa, Kenya: machine custom-embroidered Moslem cap from,
 126
Moran, the: use of red by, 18
Musical instruments
 calabash duuliga, 159
 calabash rattles, 161, 164
 carved from hardwood, 251
 hollow nuts filled with pebbles, 162
 long drums, 247

N

Natal, South Africa
 ceramic Zulu figure of woman, 58
 gourd snuff or medicinal bottle made
  by Zulus of, 163
Ndebele, the: lady's apron made of
 beads and metal chain on
 leather by, 172, 210
Necklaces and collars. See also Beads
 and beadwork; Bracelets
 of African trade beads, 213
 of amber beads, 199
 of bamboo and horn, 213
 of beads wrapped around root of the
  Muaa tree, 220
 of bone and animal teeth, 198
 brass collar from Bateke people of
  the Congo, 226
 of cowrie shells and leopard teeth,
  194
 of fourteen strands of beads, made
  by the Turkana, 221
 Kamba necklace (nzili) with aluminum pendant, 243
 Masai necklace-collars, 203, 203–4
 of ostrich shell beads, 196
 of reed, 197
 of woven beads, 215–16
  kishinda, by the Pokomo of
   Kenya, 215
  by the Pokomo, 216
  Tembu collar from the Transkei
   of South Africa, 216
 of Zulu netted beadwork, 218
Negritos (or Pygmies), 14. See also
 Pygmies
Newman, Thelma R., xiv
Ngorongoro, Tanzania: women of, doing beadwork, 204–8
Nigeria
 Awka, gates of, 227
 bead ornament of spot stitching
  from, 217
 Benin, 59
  leather fan from, 174
 carved calabashes from, 152, 153,
  154–55, 161
 ceramic water bottle made by Hausa
  from, 58
 ceremonial lidded bowl of the Yoruba, 54
 clay pots from, 53
 cowrie shells attached to raffia basket from, 196
 fly whisk adorned with beaded
  handle from, 201
 Ibadan:
  embroidery on Yoruba man's
   gown from, 122
  hamper type basket from, 144
 Igbo-Ukwu, 59
 Iwo:
  calabash carving in, 148–49
  gigantic carved calabashes from,
   152, 154–55
 Kano:
  bracelet done in lost-wax process
   in, 241
  calabash rattle from, 161
  copper tray made in, 243
  raffia basket from, 141
 leather fan from, 176
 linguist's beaded staff from, 201
 Oshogbo:
  contemporary art form, 20, 21
  fence and stairway made by Susanne Wenger for her home in,
   24–25
  indigo dyed tie-dye from, 70
 Owo: thorn carvings from, 273,
  273–82
 Oyo: preparing and carving calabashes in, 147, 149
 transition between traditional culture
  and technological invasion in, 8
 woolen weaving found in, 12
 Yoruba fan of ostrich feathers and
  beads from, 200

O

Okene cloth, 107
Olatunde, Asiru: contemporary aluminum repoussé panels made by, 244
Oshogbo, Nigeria
    contemporary art from, 20, 21
    fence and stairway made by Susanne Wenger for her home in, 24–25
    indigo dyed tie-dye from, 70
Ostrich feathers
    attached to leather, for Masai headpiece, 176
    attached to leather, for Suk wig, 176
    fan of beads and, 200
Ostrich shell beads, 195, 196
Owo, Nigeria: thorn carvings of, 273, 273–82
Oyo, Nigeria: preparing and carving calabashes in, 147, 149

P

Painting
    contemporary, 20, 21, 222, 223
    on cotton cloth, 89–96. See also Decoration of fabrics
    on leather, 186, 187, 191
Pankronu, Ghana: pots made from top down in, 31, 41–48, 49–51
Peddie in Ciskei, South Africa, 3
Plangi, 63, 69
Pokomo, the: woven beaded necklaces made by, 215, 216
Pottery
    ceramic Hausa bottle from Minna, Nigeria, 58
    ceramic Tutsi pot from Burundi, 57
    ceramic Zulu figure of woman from Natal, South Africa, 58
    ceremonial lidded bowl, 54
    clay pots from Nigeria, 53
    incised designs on pots from Bolgatanga, Ghana, 54
    Shai pots from Dodowa area of Ghana, 52
    shape and use of, 27, 56
Pottery-making
    background of, 26–27
    decorating, 48, 49

    drying, 31, 39, 43
    firing, 39, 39–40, 41, 49–51
    forming, 30–31
        pots made from bottom up, 30–31, 32–38
        pots made from top down, 31, 41–48
        tools for, 30–31, 31
    preparation of clay, 28–29, 30
Purses
    contemporary adaptation of African leatherwork, 189
    made by the Fulbe, 190
    man's shoulder-strap purse, 186–87
Pygmies, the, 14
    pipe for smoking marijuana, 252

R

Raffia baskets, 141, 142, 143, 144
Raffia weaving, 108
    bags made by the Bamileke of Cameroon, 109
    cloth garment from Yaka, Congo, 110
    loom for, 108, 108, 109
Rattles
    of calabash, 161, 164
    of hollow nuts, 162
Repoussé, 244
Resist processes. See Decoration of fabrics
Ruhengeri, Rwanda: basket tray from, 145

S

Saddlebags, leather: made by the Fulani, 166, 168
Sandals, leather, 167
Scarification, 19
Sculptures, 258. See also Wood carving
    Baluba spirit figure, 259
    carved coconut head with shell teeth, on wooden body, 259
    contemporary, 22, 24–25
    of the Makonde, 264, 264–72. See also Makonde, the
Senufo, the
    ancestor figures of, 260
    ceremonial mask of, 255
    ceremonial stick of, 258

cowrie shell belts worn by, 195
painting by, on cotton cloth, 89–96.
    See also Decoration of fabrics
Shai, the, 41
    pots of, from Dodowa area of
        Ghana, 52
Shields, leather: made by the Masai,
    166, 167
Sierra Leone: wrapped raffia basket
    from, 142
Somali: coiled basket from, 145
South Africa
    bamboo-and-horn Swazi necklace
        from, 213
    man from Peddie in Ciskei wearing
        hand-crafted jewelry and fabrics,
        3
    Ndebele lady's leather and bead-
        work apron, 172, 210
    Tembu woven bead collar, 216
    Zulus of. See Zulus
Stone sculptures, contemporary, 22
Suk, the, 15
    wig worn around arm of, made of
        ostrich feathers on leather, 176

T

Tamale, Ghana
    handwoven cotton from, 118
    leather bracelets from, 191
    village north of, 7
    weaving cooperative in, 111
Tanning, leather, 177
Tanzania
    bark cloth carpet from the Haya, 60
    beaded Masai necklace from, 221
    Makonde of. See Makonde, the
    Masai woman from, leaning against
        dung-and-clay house, 7
    Ngorongoro women doing beadwork,
        204–8
Textile arts, 59–126
    background, 59–63
    bark cloth, 59. See also Bark cloth
    designs, 61–63. See also Decoration
        of fabrics
    garments. See also Garments
        boubou worn by women of the
            Ivory Coast, 125
        embroidery on Yoruba man's gown
            from Ibadan, Nigeria, 122
        machine custom-embroidered

Moslem cap from Mombasa,
    Kenya, 126
woman's undergarment (vwuuo),
    from Korhogo, Ivory Coast, 122
materials used in, 59–60
weaving, 60–61, 102–21. See also
    Weaving
Thonging, leather, 179, 182
Thorn carvings, 273
    carving process, 274–76
    completed miniatures, 276–82
    types of thorns used, 273, 273
Timbuktu, Mali
    leather tray from, 191
    Tuareg container for storage of
        sugar, 173
Tools for art, 16
Trade beads, African, 212, 213
Trays
    of basketry, from Ruhengeri,
        Rwanda, 145
    of copper, made by heating and ham-
        mering, 243
    of leather with leather weaving, 191
Tribes, 15
Tuareg, the, 15
    decorative hanging ornaments from
        Mali, 143
    leatherwork of, 167
        man's hat, 174
        man's shoulder-strap purse, 186–
            87
        storage container for sugar, 173
    straw beads worn by, 199
Turkana, the, 15
    aluminum nose pendant from Kenya,
        242
    fourteen strand bead necklace worn
        by, 221
    ostrich shell beads worn by, 196
Tutsi, the
    large ceramic pot made by, 57
    wood and metal wrist protectors
        used by, 227
    wooden bracelet with metal inlay
        worn by, 252

U

Uganda
    Busoga: long drums made in, 247
    calabash rattle from, 164
    Kigezi: basket from, with geometric

pattern, 143
wooden-handled knife from, 250
Upper Volta
  bracelet done in lost-wax process in,
    241
  large head masks from, 256, 257,
    262
  straw basket from, 142

W

Weaving, 60–61, 102–21. See also
    Textile arts
  beads, 214, 215, 215, 216
  cleaning and spinning cotton for,
    102–3, 103–5
  cotton cloth patterns, 118, 121
  implements for, 111
  Kente cloth, 62–63, 63, 64, 65, 227
  leather on leather, 169, 186, 191,
    192
  looms used in, 60–61
    man's, 61, 110, 111–17, 119, 120
    raffia, 108, 109
    woman's, 60, 105–6, 106, 109
  nylon and polyethylene monfilament
    woven around metal bracelet
    blank, 122
  okene cloth, 107
  plastic on leather, 173
  raffia weaving. See Raffia weaving
  weaving cooperatives, 111
Weija, Ghana: pots made in, from bot-
    tom up, 30–31, 32–38, 39, 39–
    40, 41
Wenger, Susanne: fence and stairway
    made by, for her home in
    Oshogbo, Nigeria, 24–25
Wood carving
  ancestor figures, 258, 260. See also
    Sculptures
  Bambara fishing fetish, 255
  bracelet with metal inlay, 252
  canoes, 246
  carved hardwood stool from Kor-
    hogo, Ivory Coast, 249
  combs, 251
  decorations on, 263
  fetish figures, 251
  finely carved and detailed Yoruba
    box and stool, 248
  grain mortars and beer troughs, 247
  knife sheaths, 251
  large Ethiopian cowbell, 250

long drums from Busoga, Uganda,
    247
masks, 245, 246, 253, 253–57, 258.
    See also Masks
Mayobe musical instrument, 251
polishing of, 263
process of, 286, 286–89
  tools used, 286, 286, 287, 288,
    289, 290
Pygmy pipe for the smoking of mari-
    juana, 252
sculptures. See Makonde, the; Sculp-
    tures
types of wood used for, 263, 264
weaving bobbin, 250

X

Xhosa, the: man from Peddie in Ciskei
    wearing hand-crafted jewelry
    and fabrics, 3

Y

Yaka, Congo: raffia cloth garment
    from, 109
Yoruba, the, 15, 21
  ceremonial lidded bowl of, 54
  embroidery by, on man's gown, 122
  fan of ostrich feathers and beads
    made by, 200
  finely carved and detailed box and
    stool, 248
  life of, depicted on contemporary
    repoussé panels, 244
  symbols of, used in design of fence
    and stairway, 24–25

Z

Zulus, the
  beadwork of, 203
    apron from Ndebele, South Africa,
      209, 210
    girdle from South Africa, 211
    from Hlabisa, South Africa, 4
    netted beadwork necklace and
      ornaments, 218
  ceramic figure of woman, from Na-
    tal, South Africa, 58
  coiled basket by, from South Africa,
    146
  gourd snuff or medicinal bottle made
    by, in Natal, South Africa, 163